Number 115
Fall 2007

New Directions for Evaluation

Sandra Mathison
Editor-in-Chief

Using Online Surveys in Evaluation

Lois A. Ritter
Valerie M. Sue
Authors

USING ONLINE SURVEYS IN EVALUATION
Lois A. Ritter, Valerie M. Sue (authors)
New Directions for Evaluation, no. 115
Sandra Mathison, Editor-in-Chief

Copyright ©2007 Wiley Periodicals, Inc., A Wiley Company. All rights reserved. No part of this publication may be reproduced in any form or by any means, except as permitted under sections 107 and 108 of the 1976 United States Copyright Act, without either the prior written permission of the publisher or authorization through the Copyright Clearance Center, 222 Rosewood Drive, Danvers, MA 01923; (978) 750-8400; fax (978) 646-8600. The copyright notice appearing at the bottom of the first page of a chapter in this journal indicates the copyright holder's consent that copies may be made for personal or internal use, or for personal or internal use of specific clients, on the condition that the copier pay for copying beyond that permitted by law. This consent does not extend to other kinds of copying, such as copying for general distribution, for advertising or promotional purposes, for creating collective works, or for resale. Such permission requests and other permission inquiries should be addressed to the Permissions Department, c/o John Wiley & Sons, Inc., 111 River Street, Hoboken, NJ 07030; (201) 748-6011, fax (201) 748-6008, www.wiley.com/go/permissions.

Microfilm copies of issues and articles are available in 16mm and 35mm, as well as microfiche in 105mm, through University Microfilms Inc., 300 North Zeeb Road, Ann Arbor, Michigan 48106-1346.

New Directions for Evaluation is indexed in Cambridge Scientific Abstracts (CSA/CIG), Contents Pages in Education (T & F), Educational Research Abstracts Online (T & F), ERIC Database (Education Resources Information Center), Higher Education Abstracts (Claremont Graduate University), Social Services Abstracts (CSA/CIG), Sociological Abstracts (CSA/CIG), and Worldwide Political Sciences Abstracts (CSA/CIG).

NEW DIRECTIONS FOR EVALUATION (ISSN 1097-6736, electronic ISSN 1534-875X) is part of The Jossey-Bass Education Series and is published quarterly by Wiley Subscription Services, Inc., A Wiley Company, at Jossey-Bass, 989 Market Street, San Francisco, California 94103-1741.

SUBSCRIPTIONS cost $80 for U.S./Canada/Mexico; $104 international. For institutions, agencies, and libraries, $199 U.S.; $239 Canada; $273 international. Prices subject to change.

EDITORIAL CORRESPONDENCE should be addressed to the Editor-in-Chief, Sandra Mathison, University of British Columbia, 2125 Main Mall, Vancouver, BC V6T 1Z4, Canada.

www.josseybass.com

New Directions for Evaluation

Sponsored by the American Evaluation Association

EDITOR-IN-CHIEF
Sandra Mathison University of British Columbia

ASSOCIATE EDITORS
Saville Kushner University of the West of England
Patrick McKnight George Mason University
Patricia Rogers Royal Melbourne Institute of Technology

EDITORIAL ADVISORY BOARD

Michael Bamberger	Independent consultant
Gail Barrington	Barrington Research Group Inc.
Nicole Bowman	Bowman Consulting
Huey Chen	University of Alabama at Birmingham
Lois-ellin Datta	Datta Analysis
Stewart I. Donaldson	Claremont Graduate University
Michael Duttweiler	Cornell University
Jody Fitzpatrick	University of Colorado at Denver
Gary Henry	University of North Carolina, Chapel Hill
Stafford Hood	Arizona State University
George Julnes	Utah State University
Jean King	University of Minnesota
Nancy Kingsbury	US Government Accountability Office
Henry M. Levin	Teachers College, Columbia University
Laura Leviton	Robert Wood Johnson Foundation
Richard Light	Harvard University
Linda Mabry	Washington State University, Vancouver
Cheryl MacNeil	Sage College
Anna Madison	University of Massachusetts, Boston
Melvin M. Mark	The Pennsylvania State University
Donna Mertens	Gallaudet University
Rakesh Mohan	Idaho State Legislature
Michael Morris	University of New Haven
Rosalie T. Torres	Torres Consulting Group
Elizabeth Whitmore	Carleton University
Maria Defino Whitsett	Austin Independent School District
Bob Williams	Independent consultant
David B. Wilson	University of Maryland, College Park
Nancy C. Zajano	Learning Point Associates

Editorial Policy and Procedures

New Directions for Evaluation, a quarterly sourcebook, is an official publication of the American Evaluation Association. The journal publishes empirical, methodological, and theoretical works on all aspects of evaluation. A reflective approach to evaluation is an essential strand to be woven through every volume. The editors encourage volumes that have one of three foci: (1) craft volumes that present approaches, methods, or techniques that can be applied in evaluation practice, such as the use of templates, case studies, or survey research; (2) professional issue volumes that present issues of import for the field of evaluation, such as utilization of evaluation or locus of evaluation capacity; (3) societal issue volumes that draw out the implications of intellectual, social, or cultural developments for the field of evaluation, such as the women's movement, communitarianism, or multiculturalism. A wide range of substantive domains is appropriate for *New Directions for Evaluation;* however, the domains must be of interest to a large audience within the field of evaluation. We encourage a diversity of perspectives and experiences within each volume, as well as creative bridges between evaluation and other sectors of our collective lives.

The editors do not consider or publish unsolicited single manuscripts. Each issue of the journal is devoted to a single topic, with contributions solicited, organized, reviewed, and edited by a guest editor. Issues may take any of several forms, such as a series of related chapters, a debate, or a long article followed by brief critical commentaries. In all cases, the proposals must follow a specific format, which can be obtained from the editor-in-chief. These proposals are sent to members of the editorial board and to relevant substantive experts for peer review. The process may result in acceptance, a recommendation to revise and resubmit, or rejection. However, the editors are committed to working constructively with potential guest editors to help them develop acceptable proposals.

Sandra Mathison, Editor-in-Chief
University of British Columbia
2125 Main Mall
Vancouver, BC V6T 1Z4
CANADA
e-mail: nde@eval.org

CONTENTS

AUTHORS' NOTES 1
Lois A. Ritter, Valerie M. Sue

1. Introduction to Using Online Surveys 5
This introduction discusses the advantages and disadvantages of the online survey, situations when it is optimal to use the method, and how online surveys may be employed during stages of evaluation. The chapter concludes with a brief discussion of relevant ethical considerations in using online surveys in evaluation.

2. Systematic Planning for Using an Online Survey 15
This chapter outlines the evaluation planning process, focusing on how the decision to use an online survey affects choices such as selecting an evaluator, writing goals and objectives, and purchasing software.

3. Selecting a Sample 23
The unique challenges associated with selecting samples from populations for online surveys are discussed. Suggestions for choosing probability and nonprobability samples are provided.

4. Questions for Online Surveys 29
General guidelines for constructing valid and reliable survey questions are given, and the variety of question types and response formats typically found on online questionnaires is covered.

5. The Survey Questionnaire 37
Questionnaire organization, navigation, and appearance are discussed, and suggestions for formatting and layout are presented.

6. Conducting the Survey 47
Recruiting participants for online surveys via e-mail invitations and creating a Web presence are explained; techniques for increasing response rate are suggested.

7. Managing Online Survey Data 51
This chapter details the process of downloading, cleaning, and transforming online survey results in preparation for data analysis.

8. Case Studies 57
A university needs assessment survey and a statewide telemedicine project illustrate how online surveys can be incorporated into evaluation projects.

GLOSSARY 65

INDEX 67

Authors' Notes

Technology has significantly altered how evaluation research is conducted. Computing power, widespread use of the Internet among certain populations, and proliferation of businesses offering online research services have created possibilities for data collection previously unavailable to most evaluators. Among the potentialities on this new landscape is the ability to collect a vast amount of survey data quickly and inexpensively using the Internet. It is now feasible for researchers to conceive an evaluation, create a questionnaire, field an online survey, and analyze and present data all in a matter of days. The ease and speed with which online survey data can be collected and processed has untold implications for all aspects of evaluation. For example, rapid turnaround of evaluation data during a program makes it possible for service providers to make timely adjustments to program delivery so that recipients' needs are better served.

Online survey research is not without its limitations, however, and evaluators must be cautioned against letting the promise of convenient data collection guide the decision to employ an online survey when another method might be better suited to the evaluation's objectives. The advent of online survey methodology has not changed the need for a well-articulated evaluation plan including methods that are suitable to the evaluation's goals and objectives as well as to its target audience, and that are appropriate to the sponsoring organization.

The research literature surrounding online survey data collection is in its infancy and has yet to supply a set of clear guidelines or best practices for conducting Internet-based surveys. Nevertheless, it is essential that researchers who aim to use online surveys for evaluation consider the available evidence and make an informed choice to collect the most valid and reliable data possible.

The purpose of this volume is to assist evaluators in determining when an online survey is most appropriate and to guide them through the process of creating and conducting the survey. Although we do briefly review some basic concepts such as evaluation planning, research ethics, and writing good questionnaire items, we have approached this volume with the assumption that most readers are familiar with the fundamentals of survey research; we have therefore focused our attention on the particular factors relevant to conducting an online survey.

We begin this volume by discussing the conditions under which online surveys may be appropriate for evaluation. How surveys are used during the various stages of evaluation is addressed. We present a general discussion of research ethics incorporating the ethical principles developed by the American Evaluation Association (AEA) and then consider specific ethical challenges in online data collection. Special attention is given to ensuring respondents' confidentiality and anonymity in using technology to collect survey responses.

Chapter Two focuses on the planning process. Although the steps in evaluation planning are recognizable to seasoned evaluators, the special considerations introduced by using Internet-based surveys may not be. Evaluators must be technologically proficient; that is, they must be experienced with online survey software and Web-survey hosts. Organizational stakeholders must be persuaded that online data collection is feasible and appropriate, and resources for purchasing software and the services of a Web-survey host are required.

Sample selection is covered in Chapter Three. The decisions surrounding sample selection are critically important and in many cases determine if an online survey is practical for a particular evaluation project. We begin with an elementary review of populations and samples, and then we explore the options for selecting probability and nonprobability samples for online surveys. Unique ways to recruit potential respondents are suggested, and we end the chapter with a discussion of sources of error in an online survey.

Chapters Four and Five deal with the online survey questionnaire. First, we cover the essential qualities of good survey questions and discuss question types and formats for response options appropriate to online surveys. In Chapter Five, we present information about the construction of the questionnaire, including how to format and lay out the screens (questionnaire pages), paying particular attention to issues of usability and accessibility.

The next two chapters offer technical information about how to administer the survey, by e-mailing an invitation to a list of respondents or by posting the survey on a Web site. Chapter Seven covers the rudiments of how to download, clean, and transform the survey results in preparation for data analysis.

In the final chapter, we offer two case studies: a university needs assessment survey along with its follow-up and an evaluation of a statewide telemedicine project. Both successfully employed online surveys to achieve evaluation objectives. The cases are described in detail to illustrate applications of the material covered in this volume.

We hope that this volume provides useful guidance to evaluators who are contemplating use of online surveys, and that it stimulates further research into optimal strategies for collecting data using Web-based surveys.

We are grateful to Sandra Mathison and NDE Editorial Board members for their contributions and guidance. The reviewers furnished valuable suggestions, and we appreciate their thoughtful critique.

Lois A. Ritter
Valerie M. Sue
Authors

LOIS A. RITTER is an assistant professor in the nursing and health science department at California State University, East Bay. She teaches courses in community health and evaluation.

VALERIE M. SUE is an associate professor and director of the graduate program in the Department of Communication at California State University, East Bay. She teaches courses in research methods, survey research methods, statistics, and communication theory.

This chapter describes the benefits and limitations of using online surveys and the conditions under which this data collection method may be appropriate for evaluation. It also covers how online surveys can be used during stages of the evaluation process as well as ethical considerations in using this methodology.

Introduction to Using Online Surveys

Evaluation methods have drastically changed as a result of the rapid growth of the Internet and other advances in technology. A few of the ways that evaluators can use technology to gather data are to electronically track the pretest and posttest responses of participants taking an online course, gather needs assessment data using online surveys, conduct interviews using computer video software, and even hold focus groups in a real-time chat room. Using technology in evaluation can make the evaluator's job easier in some respects and more challenging in others. An online survey—one method of evaluation that uses technology—offers promising opportunities for evaluators, but it must be considered in light of the limitations of the method.

Online surveys are relatively inexpensive to conduct, have the potential to collect a lot of data quickly, and can reduce overall survey error, because the data entry chore is eliminated. On the other hand, Internet-based surveys are practical and sensible only if the target respondents have access to computer technology and the researcher has access to a list of the potential respondents. This volume provides practical information for evaluators who are considering using the Web to conduct surveys. We address the advantages and disadvantages of using the Internet to collect survey data and offer guidelines for sampling methods, creating and implementing Internet surveys, and downloading and managing data. The topics covered in this volume are of interest to evaluators in a variety of academic and professional settings who wish to consider using online surveys for data collection.

In this chapter, we begin by assessing the advantages and disadvantages of the primary methods of survey administration, paying particular attention to online surveys and the conditions under which this type of data collection method may be appropriate. We then discuss how online surveys can be used in various stages of evaluation. Finally, ethical considerations surrounding use of online surveys are presented within the context of the ethical guidelines developed by the American Evaluation Association (AEA).

When Should an Evaluator Use an Online Survey?

There are a host of factors to consider when deciding which survey method to use for an evaluation project. Each approach—sending postal mail, telephone interviewing, face-to-face interviewing, online surveying—has advantages and disadvantages. The benefits and limitations of each method should be considered in light of the evaluation's target population and objectives.

The primary advantage of the postal mail survey is its low cost, in terms of physical resources and staff time. It is possible for a lone researcher with a small budget to undertake a nationwide postal mail survey with the aid of his or her local photocopy center and post office. This attractive feature, however, must be balanced by the problems of low response rate and inability to effectively ask contingency questions, matters that plague postal mail surveys.

The ubiquity of the telephone survey is at once the method's greatest advantage and disadvantage. Its widespread use by market researchers, political pollsters, and academic investigators has led to broad acceptance of the method; however, telephone surveys also alienate many potential respondents, who often confuse legitimate research with a sales call. Additionally, the advent of caller identification, do-not-call lists, and cell-phone-only households precludes use of this method for many populations.

Face-to-face interviewing allows researchers to collect the most complex data. Contingency questions can be successfully posed, long interviews are generally tolerated, and the interviewer can note information such as the respondent's nonverbal behaviors. Of course, these rich and detailed data come at a price: face-to-face interviewing is the most expensive of the survey methods, requiring significant staff time and extended fielding of the survey.

The online survey solves many of the problems associated with the traditional survey methods; however, it is practical only for limited populations and research objectives. What follows is a discussion of the factors surrounding online surveys that should be considered before undertaking an evaluation project using this method. These factors can be divided into three categories: (1) respondent factors, (2) questionnaire factors, and (3) evaluator factors.

Respondent Factors. The respondents who participate in your survey must have access to and ability to use the Internet; ideally there is an easily attainable list of the target population, and respondents need not be bound by a particular physical location.

Internet Access. Obviously, online surveys require potential respondents to have access to the Internet and to know the rudiments of navigating the Web. If there are physical, psychological, or financial limitations to computer technology among your target population, then another technique such as telephone interviewing should be considered. An online survey works best in a situation where the respondent pool is known to have e-mail and Internet access—for example, members of a professional association or employees of a company.

Sampling Frame. A sampling frame is a list of all potential respondents to an online survey. The most efficient approach for contacting respondents is to obtain an existing e-mail list. Institutions such as universities and hospitals typically maintain e-mail lists of students and employees, for example. If no such list is available, then evaluators need to compile a sampling frame. Lack of an available sampling frame is one indication that an online survey may not be a practical choice. Evaluators should investigate the reason for the absence of an e-mail list. There are a couple of possibilities: the organization's record keeping might be lax (an annoying but manageable problem), or the members of the group you wish to survey might not have e-mail accounts or Web access (an insurmountable predicament for an online surveyor).

Geographic Location of the Participants. Because the cost of e-mailing a survey invitation across town is the same as sending it across the country (or around the world), an online survey is especially useful when the members of the population of interest are geographically dispersed. Of course, it is also convenient for surveying individuals who live or work in close proximity to one another. In this situation, however, other techniques (such as face-to-face interviewing or distributing paper-and-pencil questionnaires) are also advisable. For example, if the people from whom you wish to gather information are in your physical presence (as is the case with a training seminar), then it makes sense to distribute and collect evaluation forms in the traditional paper-and-pencil format. Note, however, that even in a situation wherein all participants are in the same location (especially if the location happens to be a computer lab), then online survey administration may still be preferable to other modes, because it eliminates the data entry chore and its associated errors.

Questionnaire Factors. The questionnaire is the instrument of data collection in an online survey. It is important to consider the type and nature of the questions that are asked and the average length of time it takes respondents to complete the questionnaire.

Types of Questions. Online surveys are effective for asking a variety of open- and closed-ended questions. Questions that require respondents to rank-order a list of items and contingency questions that ask participants to skip around in the questionnaire are generally discouraged in self-administered questionnaires. Online surveys, however, can be programmed so that respondents are not permitted to assign the same rank to two differing items, and "skip logic" can automatically take the participant to the correct place in a questionnaire. Additionally, emerging research evidence indicates that respondents tend to supply longer and more detailed answers to open-ended questions on Web-based surveys than on paper-based questionnaires (Schaefer and Dillman, 1998). Finally, online surveys offer the possibility of including images and streaming audio or video content that may enhance or lend validity to the questionnaire.

Nature of the Questions. Web-based surveys provide a measure of anonymity for survey respondents similar to that of other self-administered surveys. This affords the researcher the opportunity to probe more deeply into sensitive subjects than would be acceptable in interview surveys. The absence of an interviewer tends to free the respondents to answer personal questions more honestly than when faced with a human interviewer, whether in person or on the phone.

Length of the Questionnaire. There are two primary reasons participants abandon online surveys: technical problems, and questionnaires that are too long. Both cause respondent frustration and fatigue. In general, shorter questionnaires result in less abandonment. The appropriate length of a questionnaire should be judged relative to the target population. Samples such as employee groups and other organizational stakeholders usually tolerate longer questionnaires than do participants in a general population survey. If a lengthy questionnaire is essential for an evaluation objective and the target population is only loosely connected to the sponsoring organization, it is advisable to consider an interview method.

Evaluator Factors. The evaluator may be thought of as either the individual(s) conducting the research or the organization sponsoring the evaluation. The elements to be considered include the time frame for the evaluation project, the budget, and the evaluator's technological expertise with regard to online survey software.

Time Frame. One of the greatest features of online surveys is the potential to collect a lot of data quickly. It is possible to deploy a questionnaire one day and have collected all of your responses by the next. This is particularly useful for projects that require immediate or ongoing data collection. Projects that include an advance letter or e-mail, multiple follow-ups, or those that the evaluator may choose to keep in the field for an extended period of time do not benefit from the fast turnaround potential of online surveys.

Budget. Relative to interview methods, online surveys are economical. There are no interviewers, data entry personnel, or other staffers needed to carry out an online survey. Expenses include the cost of survey software or the services of a Web-based survey host. There is wide variation in the price of software and Web hosting, but even at the high end of the scale online surveys are reasonably priced compared to the alternative methods.

Technological Expertise. Creating and managing an online survey requires knowledge of software and data management skills. Vendors of online survey software typically offer tutorials and online help for their subscribers. Many of the popular commercial packages have a transparent interface that can be mastered in minutes. More complicated software, offering a greater variety of features, usually requires more training time on the part of the evaluator. If the evaluator does not have the technological aptitude to develop the questionnaire, then funds for a consultant must be included in the budget.

Using Online Surveys in Various Stages of Evaluation

Online surveys can be used throughout the evaluation process. They are suited to the planning and implementation phases and after the program has been completed. In this section, we give an overview of phases of the evaluation and discuss some examples of how online surveys can be used during each phase.

Evaluation is "the process of reflection whereby the value of certain actions in relation to projects, programs, or policies is assessed" (Springette, 2003, p. 264). The evaluation process consists of two stages: formative and summative. The formative stage occurs during the planning and implementation phases of the program, while the summative stage is after the program has been implemented. Evaluators tend to refer to formative and summative evaluation or process, outcome, and impact evaluation. The terms overlap, because the formative stage includes the process component, but it excludes the planning process (that is, needs assessment and pilot testing). The summative stage is made up of the outcome and impact components. Figure 1.1 shows how these terms are related.

Formative Evaluation. Formative evaluation includes the planning and implementation process. It comprises data collection done before the program begins and during the program implementation. The needs assessment, pilot test, and process evaluation (data gathered during the implementing stage) are parts of the formative evaluation process.

Needs Assessment. Needs assessment is a procedure designed to gather data about the needs of the people who are going to be served by the program or intervention. Online surveys can be useful for gathering data from a closed population, which can be thought of as one whose size and composition are fixed in the time during which the research takes place. Examples are the students who are housed on campus at a university,

Figure 1.1. Comparison of Evaluation Terms

Formative	Summative	
Process	Outcome	Impact

Source: Adapted from McKenzie, Neiger, and Smeltzer (2005).

the employees of an engineering firm, or the members of a professional organization.

An Internet-based survey also can be used as a pretest to identify gaps in knowledge and current beliefs. For example, an evaluator responsible for determining the effectiveness of an educational campaign aimed at reducing the cholesterol level among those exposed to campaign messages might first survey the selected participants to test their knowledge about high- and low-cholesterol foods. This baseline data would be used as a source of comparison during and at the end of the campaign to test for change in respondents' knowledge.

Using online surveys in open populations is more challenging, because there is no readily available e-mail list of such a population. It is not impossible, however. In a situation of this kind, the evaluator must rely on nonprobability sampling methods (see Chapter Three, on sampling, later in this volume), thus limiting the external validity of the results. Say, for example, that a community group wants to assess the need for a public-access television station in its city. An online needs-assessment survey could be placed on the city Web site; anyone visiting the site would be eligible to participate. Although not ideal in terms of representative responses, the data would constitute a good starting place for further research or perhaps make up one component in a multimethod data collection approach.

Pilot Testing. During pilot testing, evaluators test the intervention or evaluation instruments by gathering information from the members served or affected by the intervention, or professionals in the field. Online surveys can be useful if you are pilot-testing an online course or Web site, e-mailing an instrument for review, or asking opinions about a new educational brochure posted on a site. They are less useful in pilot-testing workshops in a classroom or educational brochures for the general population (or a population that tends to not use or have access to the Internet, for example).

Process Evaluation. Process evaluation is conducted during the implementation phase of a program. This is where necessary changes in program delivery can be identified for implementation before the program ends. Online surveys can be constructive during this stage; for example, asking facilitators about the quality and usefulness of a new course while it is being given might yield data indicating that the content is not suitable for the audience. There would be time to revise the program content to make it a better match for the audience.

Summative Evaluation. Summative evaluation uses data collected at the end of a program to assess the outcomes and impacts of the intervention.

Outcome Evaluation. Outcome evaluation focuses on the immediate benefits of the program and its effect on the target audience—for example, an increase in knowledge or change in skill level. Online surveys can be used effectively to conduct posttests of program participants. If an evaluator wants to estimate the impact of a smoking cessation campaign, he or she can use an online survey to question participants about changes in their smoking behavior or attitude toward cigarettes, or about their knowledge of coping mechanisms at the end of the campaign period. Internet surveys are less useful in outcome evaluation when the variables to be tested involve physiological measures such as respiration rate or a report of blood pressure. Respondents are unlikely to have the necessary equipment to report this information accurately.

Impact Evaluation. Impact evaluation measures the long-term effects of the program, which is often the ultimate objective of an intervention. Online surveys are effective for longitudinal research that involves repeated contact with the same respondents. For example, if you want to know whether participants in a new diet program maintain their weight three, six, and nine months after the program ends, online surveys are a convenient way to recontact the participants to ask them about their eating habits and their weight. Online surveys may not be useful if you are concerned that your target audience is somewhat transient and might change e-mail addresses frequently. For a highly mobile sample, an online survey faces the same threat to internal validity—that is, participant attrition—as do other longitudinal techniques.

Ethical Considerations

Ethics is an important consideration in conducting evaluations, and there are issues unique to online surveys that should be considered. The American Evaluation Association AEA has developed five guiding principles for evaluators: systematic inquiry, competence, integrity and honesty, respect for people, and responsibilities for general and public welfare (American Evaluation Association, 2004). Evaluators can download the guidelines from the AEA Web site (see reference list entry). We discuss three specific ethical concerns contained within the five AEA guiding principles related to using online surveys: (1) informed consent, (2) ensuring respondent confidentiality and anonymity, and (3) ethical interpretation and reporting of results.

Informed Consent and Confidentiality and Anonymity. In almost all cases, respondents to online surveys are volunteers. The related AEA principle is respect for people. The principle encompasses this statement: "Evaluators should abide by current professional ethics, standards, and regulations regarding risks, harms, and burdens that might befall those participating in the evaluation; regarding informed consent for participation in evaluation; and regarding informing participants and clients about the scope and limits of confidentiality" (American Evaluation Association, 2004).

To make an informed decision about participating in the evaluation, volunteers should be briefed on (1) the overarching purpose of the survey, especially if sensitive or potentially embarrassing information is addressed; (2) the identity of the evaluator or evaluation team; (3) how the data are to be used; (4) the average length of time to complete the survey, and if respondents will be contacted in the future with additional surveys; and (5) whether there are any risks involved in participating in the survey, such as asking respondents to disclose uncomfortable or embarrassing information.

This information can be conveyed in the e-mail survey invitation or as part of the introduction to the questionnaire. An institutional review board (IRB) generally does not require a signed consent form for participants in a survey; in fact, it would be nearly impossible to get signed consent forms in online surveys. If you believe that your survey may pose any physical or psychological threat to respondents, you should consult with the appropriate IRB representative at your institution to ensure that the research protocol includes appropriate safeguards to protect participants.

Perhaps one of the most rigorous requirements in research is preserving the participant's confidentiality. Frequently, the respondents to your survey expect that the information they furnish will be confidential—that is, neither the fact of their participation nor the information they give is to be disclosed to third parties. If you have promised confidentiality, you have an ethical responsibility to ensure that participants' identification and information is protected. If you cannot (or will not) prevent disclosure of respondent information, you must make this fact abundantly clear in the invitation to participate in the online survey so that respondents have the opportunity to refuse participation.

The promise of anonymity is often included in the same sentence that guarantees confidentiality, almost as if the two concepts were the same. The statement typically reads "All your responses will remain strictly confidential and anonymous." Unfortunately, many people forget that anonymity extends beyond not requiring names and addresses on a questionnaire. Technically, a response to an e-mail survey is never truly anonymous, because evaluators know the respondent's e-mail address. Even without this information, it is easy to attach identifying code numbers to questionnaires or link survey numbers to a database containing respondent information. As a result, many potential respondents are skeptical of electronic surveys offering anonymity. The important fact here is not that researchers *must* promise anonymity. What is essential is that if the promise is made, the researcher is obligated to take the necessary steps to ensure that identifying information about survey respondents is kept separate from their responses.

Additionally, even if survey respondents know that their anonymity is not guaranteed (as when you say you may contact the respondent again for follow-up information), you have a responsibility to the respondent to guarantee that subsequent contact is appropriate. For example, do not tell a potential respondent that he or she may be contacted to gather more information when you are actually selling the name to a telemarketing company. This same rule applies when you are gathering e-mail addresses from potential participants. For example, if you are at a community event and you ask attendees to participate in an evaluation of the event via e-mail and get their e-mail addresses, then the addresses should be used only for the stated purpose; hence they should not be sold, shared, or used for solicitation for other activities.

Ethical Interpretation and Reporting of Results

Data interpretation and reporting are fraught with ethical dilemmas for evaluators. Reference to ethical data handling can be found in all five of AEA's guiding principles, specifically AEA notes: "Evaluators should not misrepresent their procedures, data, or findings. Within reasonable limits, they should attempt to prevent or correct misuse of their work by others" (American Evaluation Association, 2004).

In reporting survey results, one encounters a host of situations that can potentially jeopardize respondent confidentiality and accurate interpretation and presentation of evaluation results. In gathering demographic information that can identify respondents, the evaluator has an obligation not to produce reports that can lead to identification of individuals. For example, in an employee survey it is reasonable to ask about gender and ethnic background to ensure that the needs of all employees are being met. If this information is gathered, be careful not to generate a report that can lead to identification of individual employees (if providing information at the department level, do not present the data such that, say, the only female employee under age twenty-five can be identified). A reasonable rule of thumb to avoid this problem is to produce results only for groups containing at least ten individuals. This way, no individual can be singled out.

Data interpretation can present another set of problematic issues for survey researchers. Efforts should be made to fully and accurately represent the results gathered by the survey. Too often, people do not present enough information about the procedures used for gathering the data, the sampling strategy, the error and confidence levels, the response rate, or how the data were analyzed. Without this information, it is easy to misinterpret the results or overinterpret some findings, which will lead to erroneous conclusions.

Another situation arises when evaluators are asked not to report data that present the host organization unfavorably. As was already mentioned, every effort should be made to present the results of the survey completely and accurately. This may mean presenting some information that suggests areas of discord or opportunities for improvement. These results should not be hidden, or simply forgotten. Doing so is a disservice to the organization and the people who responded to the survey (not to mention questionable ethics). If you are hired as an evaluation consultant, then you should ask, in advance, how the results will be disseminated, favorable or not. The AEA addresses this issue well:

> If evaluators determine that certain procedures or activities are likely to produce misleading evaluative information or conclusions, they have the

responsibility to communicate their concerns and the reasons for them. If discussions with the client do not resolve these concerns, the evaluator should decline to conduct the evaluation. If declining the assignment is unfeasible or inappropriate, the evaluator should consult colleagues or relevant stakeholders about other proper ways to proceed. (Options might include discussions at a higher level, a dissenting cover letter or appendix, or refusal to sign the final document.) [American Evaluation Association, 2004]

Summary

Online surveys are not appropriate for all evaluation efforts, but they are appropriate in many circumstances. Evaluators need to consider their advantages and disadvantages, who they are attempting to gather data from, the geographic location of the population, and time and budget constraints. As with any research methodology, the evaluation process needs to be carried out in an ethical manner. Evaluators are expected to be competent to conduct the evaluation and be honest and respectful of those who are involved in the evaluation process, the stakeholders, and the general public.

References

American Evaluation Association. *Guiding Principles for Evaluators* (2004). Retrieved Nov. 24, 2006, from http://www.eval.org/Publications/GuidingPrinciples.asp.

McKenzie, J., Neiger, B., and Smeltzer, J. *Planning, Implementing and Evaluating Health Promotion Programs.* San Francisco: Pearson/Benjamin Cummings, 2005.

Schaefer, R., and Dillman, D. A. "Development of a Standard E-mail Methodology: Results of an Experiment." *Public Opinion Quarterly*, 1998, 62(3), 378–397.

Springette, J. "Issues in Participatory Evaluation." In M. Minkler and N. Wallerstein (eds.), *Community-Based Participatory Research for Health.* San Francisco: Jossey-Bass, 2003.

2

This chapter describes the overall planning process for using online surveys in your evaluation and how to choose survey software or a Web host for your evaluation project.

Systematic Planning for Using an Online Survey

Evaluations are conducted for numerous reasons, among them to gather information about community needs, evaluate quality of instruction, or assess the impact of an advertising campaign. Every evaluation differs, but they all require a systematic plan if the goals of the project are to be achieved. Conducting an evaluation is a process, and one that includes several steps.

The general steps in conducting an evaluation using an online survey are the same as in using other methods: planning, data collection, data analysis, reporting, and application (McKenzie, Neiger, and Smeltzer, 2005). Each of these general step includes a series of related tasks. The process is outlined in Figure 2.1.

We have presented the evaluation process as linear in Figure 2.1, with the arrows moving in only one direction; but it is important to note that movement within the process is not always unidirectional. Every step has an impact on the other ones. The stakeholders' interests affect the evaluation objectives, evaluation objectives partly determine the format of the survey, the format determines the question types and response categories that are used, the question types determine the kind of data gathered, the kind of data guides the data analysis methods used, and data analysis outcomes cycle back to the evaluation objectives. All of these steps are constrained by resources, laws, program structures and policies, and ethics.

Figure 2.1. Steps in the Evaluation Process

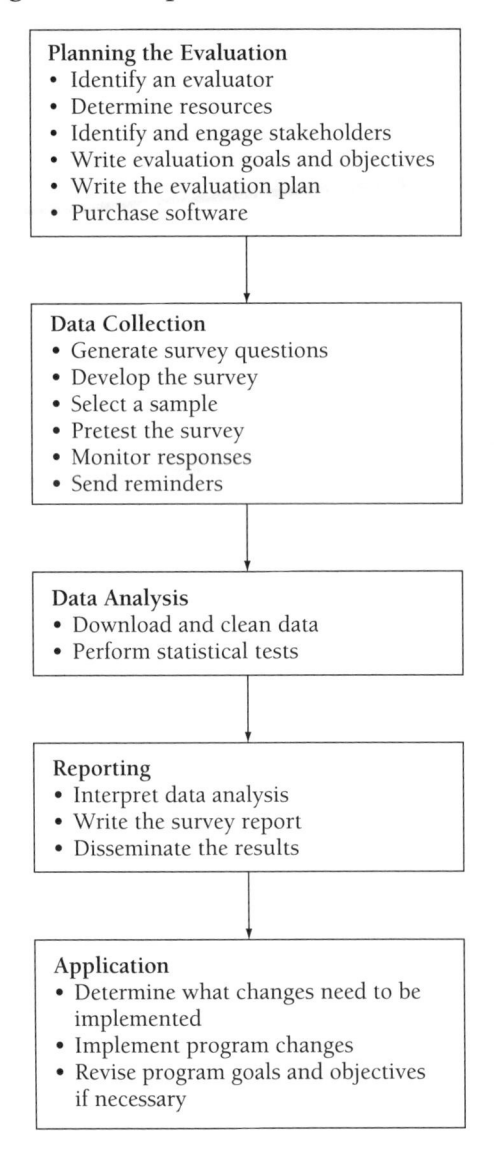

Planning the Evaluation
- Identify an evaluator
- Determine resources
- Identify and engage stakeholders
- Write evaluation goals and objectives
- Write the evaluation plan
- Purchase software

Data Collection
- Generate survey questions
- Develop the survey
- Select a sample
- Pretest the survey
- Monitor responses
- Send reminders

Data Analysis
- Download and clean data
- Perform statistical tests

Reporting
- Interpret data analysis
- Write the survey report
- Disseminate the results

Application
- Determine what changes need to be implemented
- Implement program changes
- Revise program goals and objectives if necessary

Even though the process of evaluation using Internet-based surveys begins in a familiar manner, the unique requirements of the online methodology become apparent almost immediately in choosing an evaluator, requiring special consideration as you make your way through the planning process. In this chapter, we review the steps in the evaluation planning process, paying particular attention to the challenges and opportunities presented by using online surveys for evaluation. We conclude with a discussion of the factors involved in selecting appropriate software for conducting online surveys.

Identify an Evaluator

In addition to the usual requirements that the investigator be experienced in evaluation strategies generally and survey methodology particularly, in selecting a candidate for an evaluation project that employs an online survey it is important to investigate the candidates' technological expertise. Project considerations such as complexity of the evaluation and time allotted for it also determine the type of researcher hired for a project. Large and complex projects that must be completed in a short amount of time require evaluators who have substantial experience using online survey software and their associated data analysis packages. It is less important to seek out an experienced online survey researcher for a simple evaluation that can be completed using a widely available, easy-to-use commercial software package.

Identify and Engage the Stakeholders

The stakeholders are the people who have an interest in your program and hence are the primary users of your evaluation. They may include the funding agency, managers, the general public, or the people who deliver the program (that is, trainers). You will want to engage them to improve the credibility of your program and evaluation, increase the likelihood that the lessons learned from the evaluation will be used to make changes, avoid conflict of interest, improve the quality and comprehensiveness of the evaluation, protect the interests of the people involved in the program and evaluation, clarify the roles and responsibilities of people involved, and get buy-in and approval of the evaluation plan. Most important, involving the stakeholders increases the chances that the evaluation results are read and used by the decision makers. With regard to using online surveys, ensure that the stakeholders are comfortable and supportive of using this methodology and that they understand the benefits and limitations associated with the method.

Determine Resources

Resources include staff and consultant's time, technology, equipment, information, buildings, funds, and other assets you need in implementing your evaluation plan. The decision to employ an online survey requires purchase of software and perhaps a monthly fee for the services of a Web host. Software prices vary widely, from free to tens of thousands of dollars. Expenses associated with the purchase of software or Web hosting fees are usually offset by savings in materials and staff time. There are no printing or postage costs, and online surveys do not require interviewers, call centers, or data-entry personnel.

Write Goals and Objectives

Writing evaluation goals and objectives for an online survey is similar to writing goals and objectives when other methods are used. As with other methods, it is necessary to consider if the goals of the project are achievable by using an online survey. Methodology should not drive objectives, so be sure that your objectives are written to match the needs and interests of the stakeholders and other interested parties and are not guided by your desire to conduct an online survey.

Write the Evaluation Plan

Your evaluation plan describes how the evaluation will be conducted. It must take into consideration the resources, stakeholder interests, and goals and objectives. The plan may change as the evaluation unfolds and information is gathered. It includes information about the purpose of the evaluation, program and participant descriptions, goals and objectives, evaluation questions, data collection methods, limitations of the evaluation, a timeline, data analysis procedures, and dissemination methods. Most of these components have already been discussed, with the exception of the timeline and data collection methods. Data collection methods are discussed in the next four chapters, so this leaves the issue of a timeline.

In your timeline, you must add some extra time for developing the online survey if your evaluator has limited experience with the software you are going to use. One the other hand, you need less time for data collection because the responses are gathered faster than when a survey is mailed or interviews are conducted. Other areas that take less time are data entry and possibly data analysis.

Select Software for Your Evaluation Project

To conduct a Web-based survey, you have two options: you may subscribe to the services of a Web-based survey host, or you can purchase online survey software to be used locally on your computer and host the survey on your own Web site. With either approach, there are an overwhelming number of choices. The first option, using Web-based survey hosts (also known as application service providers or ASPs), gives the user a range of services, including the ability to create questionnaires, disseminate and track the surveys, analyze data, and create graphs, all using the Web site of the survey host. Zoomerang and SurveyMonkey are two Web-based survey management tools that are commonly used because of their simplicity and low cost. Many of the ASPs offer limited, trial versions of their services for potential customers to test. The second option is to purchase software and install it on the evaluator's computer; the evaluator creates the questionnaire offline and uploads it to a Web site or e-mails it to respondents. This option leaves evaluators responsible for installing the software and supplying their own technical expertise and support.

Regardless of which option you choose, the challenge comes in selecting appropriate software and a Web survey host for your needs and level of technical expertise. Because new software programs and Web-based hosts appear on the market frequently, it is not advantageous for us to describe specific vendors; Table 2.1 shows a small sample of online survey software vendors and service providers. We address some general considerations in choosing software and a survey host.

Cost. The cost of survey software and ASPs ranges widely. Some are free but usually place a limit on the number and type of surveys available to users. Many offer reasonably priced monthly or annual subscriptions. A few create custom software and handle Web hosting, at a substantial cost to the user. More expensive programs tend to have more features than less expensive options; this does not necessarily render them superior. The important task for the evaluator is to find the least expensive product that gives all of the features needed to conduct an evaluation effectively. Expensive software packages loaded with options that you are unlikely to use are not cost-efficient and slow down the process, because it takes longer to become proficient with the software than if a simpler option is chosen. Unless you are conducting an evaluation with unique questionnaire options, special formatting requirements, or complex data analysis, off-the-shelf

Table 2.1. A Sample of Online Survey Vendors

Company	Web Address
Cool Surveys	coolsurveys.com
EZSurvey	raosoft.com
Infopoll	infopoll.com
Inquisite	inquisite.com
InSite	insitesurveys.com
InstantSurvey	instantsurvey.com
LiveSurveys	livesurveys.com
PollPro	pollpro.com
StatPac	statpac.com
SuperSurvey	supersurvey.com
Survey System	surveysystem.com
SurveyCrafter	surveycarfter.com
SurveyGold	surveygold.com
SurveyMonkey	surveymonkey.com
SurveySaid	surveysaid.com
SurveyTrends	surveytrends.com
Zoomerang	zoomerang.com

products (as opposed to custom software packages) will probably suit your needs.

User-friendliness. Purchase survey software with an intuitive structure that does not require long training time or technical skills that are not within the reach or interest of the evaluator. Wizards and design templates can assist users with developing the questionnaire. If you intend to use the same survey more than once (say, for a pretest and posttest of knowledge), be sure that the program has the capability for the evaluator to create a template and then reuse the survey as needed. Some programs have libraries with common survey questions, such as demographic items. These question libraries can be helpful to survey developers, and they can reduce the survey development time.

Issues Related to Questions and Response Options. Investigate the ability to use a variety of response options: radio buttons, check boxes, matrix responses, and open-ended questions. Also, look into the ability for the respondent to select one or more responses to a question and if you have the ability to use Likert-type or other common attitude scale responses. Another feature to consider is the capability of participants to skip questions (forcing respondents to answer a question can lead to a high dropout rate) as well as the ability to include contingency questions. They allow you to direct the set of questions that are presented to the respondent according to his or her response to a previous question. This enables the evaluator to tailor the survey to the participant or situation. For example, if you have a three-day training, you may have some questions for a participant who attended only the first day and another set for a person who attended all three days. This feature is also useful if you are going to have your survey available in more than one language; for the first question, the respondent can select the language in which he or she prefers to complete the survey and the program then directs the person to the survey written in the desired language.

Limitations and Appearance. Some of the less expensive software packages and Web hosts impose a limit on the number of questions that can be asked and the number of respondents that may be contacted. The same may be done with the ability to use tables, images, audio, video, or ALT tags (see the Glossary) on the survey. If your evaluation survey is short and simple with a small sample, then these limitations may not pose any problems. If you plan to use long questionnaires or survey large samples of respondents, you should seek out software without such limits. In terms of appearance, inquire about available aesthetic options for color, logos, and font styles and sizes. This is particularly important if you have an audience with special needs, such as senior citizens who might require questionnaires presented in a 14 point font.

Sampling Options. For most evaluation projects, you will probably have a list of e-mail addresses that you want to send the survey to, but this is not always the case (for example, a community needs assessment project does not typically have a readily available list of potential respondents). If you do not have an e-mail distribution list, then you can purchase one. Zoomerang, for example, allows you to purchase lists depending on a variety of characteristics, such as language spoken at home, dining patterns, or socioeconomic status.

Disseminating Your Survey. Seek out a program that enables you to easily import your e-mail distribution list from another program. Once you have disseminated the surveys, you may want to track who has responded so that you can send out follow-up e-mails to increase the response rate. If so, then select a program that has this capability. Another feature to look for is the ability to limit responses to one per person. This can be done by assigning passwords to selected respondents or by identifying the Internet provider (IP) addresses of the respondents. Once your respondent has completed and submitted the survey, you can thank them for taking time to complete the questionnaire. See if your software program allows you to distribute thank-you notes automatically as respondents complete the questionnaires.

Data Analysis Capabilities. Obviously, you will want to analyze the data you have collected in a manner that enables you to address your evaluation objectives and meet the needs of your stakeholders. The complexity of your data analysis depends on your objectives. In some cases, simple descriptive statistics are all that is needed, and most survey programs offer this level of analysis on their Web sites. For more complex calculations, assess the options for downloading your data directly into a statistical program such as SPSS or SAS. If the program exports the data only to Microsoft Excel, this may be acceptable, because most data analysis packages import Excel spreadsheets easily. For evaluators who conduct complex data analysis frequently, an all-inclusive package may be the best approach. STATPAC, for example, offers a reasonably priced product that includes software to create e-mail and Web-based surveys and conduct basic and advanced statistical analysis (including analysis of open-ended survey questions), as well as free Web hosting of surveys.

Sharing Data. There are times when you will want others to be able to view the results, as they are collected. Say you are an external evaluator and the people at the training site want to view the needs assessment data so they can tailor their training to meet the needs of the attendees; you would want them to be able to access those data at any time. Many Web hosts have this feature and give the survey developer the option to share results using a URL to enable the interested party to view the results. The developer can send the URL to the people with whom he or she wants to share the results or post the URL on a Web site. Web-based survey hosts, such as SurveyMonkey and Zoomerang, allow the survey developer to share the results at a number of levels of security. If using Zoomerang, the evaluator can elect to keep results private or share them in one of two ways: (1) restricted (results are shared, but individual responses are kept private) or (2) public (all results, including individual responses, are shared).

Access for All. If your target population has a disability such as a visual impairment, find a program that can create accessible surveys for the visually impaired. WebSurvey, for example, can accommodate respondents who use screen readers. If language differences are an issue, select a program such as Zoomerang, which can translate a survey and the responses into forty-two languages for an additional fee.

Multiple Users. A major concern might be that you have multiple people needing to use the Web host simultaneously. In some cases, if you purchase an account with a Web host you have to pay for each additional user. Other hosts allow you to have an unlimited number of users with only one account. This latter approach keeps costs down, which is often a concern with an evaluation budget. If multiple members of the evaluation team need access to the Web host at the same time, it is important to investigate the vendor's account restrictions.

Security. Password protection prevents people who are not part of your target audience from completing your survey. This is important if you are targeting a specific group and you do not want people outside the group to complete the survey.

Customer Service. Explore whether the Web host or software program has customer support service available (if it is a phone service, explore the typical waiting time). Also, what kinds of training options are there? Is there a manual or a tutorial? (Adapted from Sue and Ritter, 2007.)

Summary

In this chapter, we have touched on a general approach to conducting an evaluation while focusing more specifically on the planning process. We have described items to consider in selecting your software or Web survey host. There are hundreds of Web-based hosts and survey software programs to select from; you need to consider your evaluation budget and objectives and the evaluator's technological capabilities and experience with using online surveys. The next major step in the evaluation process is data collection, which includes selecting your sample; this is the subject of Chapter Three.

References

McKenzie, J., Neiger, B., and Smeltzer, J. *Planning, Implementing and Evaluating Health Promotion Programs.* San Francisco: Pearson/Benjamin Cummings, 2005.
Sue, V., and Ritter, L. *Conducting Online Surveys.* Thousand Oaks, Calif.: Sage, 2007.

In this chapter, we begin our discussion about data collection with the focus on selecting a sample. Sample types are explained, and concerns related to sampling in using online surveys are discussed.

Selecting a Sample

In this chapter, we give an overview of sampling methods that are appropriate for conducting online surveys. We begin with a basic discussion of populations and samples and then move into a more specific treatment of sampling strategies.

The choice of respondents recruited to complete your survey should be based on your evaluation objectives and the identified target audience; in other words, what is the population that you want to make generalizations about based on your survey results? In some cases the answer is straightforward. For example, if you want to assess the instructional methods used in a course, then your sample will be drawn from the list of course participants. But in other cases the answer may not be so apparent. If you want to assess the impact of a new policy on a community, it may be more difficult to determine who has felt the impact of the policy, and it is unlikely that you will have a list of every member of the community.

Populations and Samples

A population is a group of persons, institutions, events, or objects that the evaluator wishes to describe or make predictions about; a sample is a group of participants selected from a larger group (population) in hopes that studying the smaller group will yield information about the larger group. The goal is to select a sample that is representative of the population of interest.

In many evaluation projects, evaluators and other stakeholders are interested in the opinions, attributes, or changes in behavior or knowledge of people who participate in the program to help them assess the strengths and weaknesses of the program or service and its effectiveness. When an evaluator writes objectives, he or she already has a specific population in mind. You are conducting a census when you gather data from every member of the population; in most research situations conducting a population census is prohibitively expensive or impossible. For example, say you are interested in assessing the eating behaviors of university sophomores. You could not possibly gather data from every sophomore in the United States in a timely manner. Online surveys provide one of the few opportunities for researchers to conduct a census economically; the cost of e-mailing a survey link to ten thousand individuals is no greater than it would be to e-mail the same message to a thousand. Moreover, direct data entry of responses by the participants eliminates what would be a labor-intensive data-entry chore for the evaluation staff.

After you have identified your population, you need to acquire or create a comprehensive population list—that is, a sampling frame. Examples of sampling frames are a list of students who attend a school, people who registered for a course, or people who use a service at a specified facility. Your frame includes people who are eligible to participate in the evaluation (as with course attendees) and those who are not eligible (such as males in a study about premenstrual syndrome). Sampling frames may have to be segmented so that only eligible participants are sampled for the survey.

Now you are ready to select your sample from your population. Recall that a sample is a subset of the population. For example, by asking a group of one hundred patients about their experience with the staff at a hospital, an evaluator may be able to make inferences about the quality of patient services at the hospital. This type of inference making, however, can be done only if the sample was generated randomly.

Open and Closed Populations

A closed population is one whose size and composition is fixed at a particular point in time. Closed populations, such as employee or membership groups, typically have a list of their constituents. The researcher's task when working with a closed population is to obtain the population list that serves as a sampling frame. An open population is fluid, membership is constantly changing, and there is generally no easily attainable population list. Open populations are more challenging because before sampling can commence a sampling frame must be constructed by the evaluator.

Samples for Online Surveys

There are two categories of survey samples: probability and nonprobability. Probability samples are generated when every individual in the population has a known chance of being selected to participate in the evaluation; nonprobability samples, on the other hand, are selected on the basis of the respondents' availability or the researcher's judgment. In this case, the chance of each respondent being included in the sample is not known. If the goal of the research is to generalize the results to the underlying population, then a probability sample is required. Say you want to assess whether people who received an influenza shot at your clinic got the flu. A sample can be randomly selected from a list of all of the people who came to the clinic to get a flu shot. Using a probability sample does not guarantee that your estimate accurately reflects the population characteristics you wish to evaluate, but it is a necessary condition for generalizing to a population.

Probability Samples. If a sampling frame is readily available or can be easily created, then probability sampling using one of the standard techniques (simple random sampling, systematic random sampling, stratified sampling, or cluster sampling) can be employed.

To randomly sample from a population for which there is no sampling frame, there are three options: a multimethod approach, a prerecruited panel, or intercept sampling.

Multimethod Approach. The multimethod approach entails inviting people to participate in the evaluation by telephone (using random-digit dialing) or postal mail, and instructing them about how to access the online survey. This clearly takes more time than simply e-mailing a survey invitation with a link to a list of potential participants. Follow-up mailings encouraging participation also may be necessary to ensure an adequate sample size.

Prerecruited Panels. The second alternative is to use prerecruited panels. Given enough time, a researcher could construct a prerecruited panel by first contacting randomly selected potential respondents by telephone or postal mail and inviting them to participate in future online surveys. Once the panel is assembled, the evaluator can randomly select participants from the panel for a particular survey.

Another option is to use a commercial research service. One example is Knowledge Networks (www.knowledgenetworks.com), which maintains an Internet panel that represents the full spectrum of Internet and non-Internet households. Their participant list includes tens of thousands of people who are randomly recruited by telephone (using random-digit dialing). Households that do not have Internet access when they are contacted are given the necessary hardware and free Web access. Nonresponse is usually lower with this type of group, because they have previously agreed to participate and may be getting paid to do so. A major advantage to the prerecruited panel is that you can detect sample bias by comparing respondents with nonrespondents to see if any particular characteristics significantly differ. Of course, the use of commercial services such as this one adds substantially to the evaluation budget.

Intercept Sampling. A final strategy uses pop-up messages on Web sites to invite visitors to participate in the survey. The pop-ups can be programmed to appear every time a unique user enters the site; or systematically, for every nth user; or randomly. Some site visitors find this practice annoying and may even leave the site in response to a pop-up message. Incentives can help to increase response rate.

Nonprobability Samples. The chance of an individual's selection for inclusion in a nonprobability sample cannot be computed. Respondents are selected on the basis of convenience or availability. Convenience samples for online surveys can be generated by posting a survey on a frequently visited Web site. For example, a community needs assessment questionnaire might be posted on a city's Web page. Any visitor to the site may elect to complete the survey. A convenience sample also can be generated by advertising, typically with the offer of an incentive, either on a Web site or in other media.

It is possible to purchase a list of potential participants from a Web survey host. Zoomerang, for example, maintains a panel of 2.5 million opt-in survey volunteers. A sample of these participants can be selected according to any standard demographic or psychographic criteria the researcher desires. This type of volunteer panel should not be confused with the prerecruited panel mentioned earlier. Whereas the latter represents a randomly selected group of online and offline participants (respondents who are not selected are not permitted to participate), the opt-in panel is composed of individuals who have self-selected into the panel (anyone can participate).

Finally, the nonprobability technique of "snowball sampling" can be used effectively in Web-based surveys. To assemble a snowball sample, the evaluator need only find a few respondents who meet the inclusion criteria and persuade them to participate; those initial participants are then asked to refer other individuals for the survey. It is customary to offer an incentive for each referral. This technique is frequently used when it is difficult to locate a population or when homogeneity of the sample is the desired outcome.

Sample Size

Perhaps the most frequently posed question in all of survey research is, "How large does my sample need to be?" There is no simple answer to this query. The researcher must consider the type of sample he or she is using. Appropriate sample sizes for a particular margin of error and confidence level can be computed provided that a probability sample is to be employed. For instance, at the 95 percent confidence level a sample size of 384 respondents will guarantee a maximum 5 percent margin of error in estimating a population proportion. Sample size calculators are widely available on the Internet and are easy to use. The only caveat is that the calculations work on the assumption that some sort of probability sample is used.

If a nonprobability sample is used for the evaluation, the researcher will not be able to use a calculator to determine sample size. No formulas for statistical inference exist for estimating sample size with nonprobability samples, because it is not possible to know the likelihood of any particular participant being selected for the sample. Guidelines that have been suggested for determining a suitable sample size for nonprobability samples include (1) somewhere between thirty and five hundred, (2) about 10 percent of the parent population, and (3) the largest sample you can afford (Alreck and Settle, 1995; Hill, 1998).

The factors influencing how many participants to include in a probability or nonprobability sample often boil down to budget and time. If incentives are offered for completing the survey, then the number of respondents is determined by the amount of money allocated for participant incentives. Deadlines for data reporting are also a primary consideration; if the deadline is imminent then the survey will remain in the field for a short amount of time, thus generating relatively fewer responses than if the survey is allowed to remain available to potential respondents for a longer period.

Nonresponse Bias

The sample selected from the population is not necessarily the group who actually complete the survey. The reality is that no matter how persuasive your appeal, not everyone whom you invite to participate in your online survey will respond. The people who are asked to participate and do not are referred to as nonrespondents. In addition, you will have dropouts—people who start to take the survey but do not complete it. It is important to note that there may be certain characteristics of the nonrespondents and the dropouts that are relevant to the decisions made from the evaluation results. For example, people who were unsatisfied with a course or students with lower-than-average literacy skills may fail to respond to a survey in greater numbers than those who achieved success with the course. By making inferences about the course on the basis of the respondent data alone, an evaluator may overestimate the student satisfaction level because only those who were satisfied responded to the survey.

The problem of nonresponse can take two forms: *unit* nonresponse, where the respondent does not participate in the survey at all; and *item* nonresponse, where the respondent skips particular questions on the survey. Unit nonresponse is calculated by dividing the number of individuals who fail to respond by the total number of potential participants invited to complete the survey.

Item nonresponse can be assessed by examining the number of missing values on each survey question. Almost all questions contain a few missing values; that is, not every respondent answers every question. If you find that a large number of respondents skipped a particular question, then the question should be reviewed for clarity and proper functioning (perhaps there was a technical error). Pilot-testing your instrument can help prevent this from occurring.

Couper (2000) outlined three explanations for low response rate in Internet surveys: (1) the motivation tools used in mail or phone surveys cannot be used in the same way for online surveys, and analogous techniques have not yet been developed; (2) technical difficulties may prevent some respondents from starting to answer questionnaires or cause them to abandon the survey halfway; and (3) concerns about the confidentiality of e-mail responses discourage some prospective participants. With these considerations in mind, it behooves evaluators to be creative in offering incentives to online survey participants. Be vigilant about pretesting survey questionnaires, ensuring that they function properly and are easy to navigate; and take steps to protect respondent confidentiality whenever possible.

Summary

In this chapter, we have reviewed some of the basic concepts relevant to online survey sampling, presented some probability and nonprobability techniques for selecting a sample, and briefly discussed sample size determination and nonresponse bias. Although some standard survey sampling techniques (such as simple random sampling) may be employed for online surveys, the particular challenges of finding an adequate sampling frame for many populations makes it necessary for researchers to explore alternate avenues, such as using multiple methods or prerecruited panels.

References

Alreck, P. L., and Settle, R. B. *The Survey Research Handbook* (2nd ed.). Chicago: Irwin, 1995.

Couper, M. P. "Web Surveys: A Review of Issues and Approaches." *Public Opinion Quarterly,* 2000, 64(4), 464–494.

Hill, R. "What Sample Size Is 'Enough' in Internet Survey Research?" *Interpersonal Computing and Technology: An Electronic Journal for the 21st Century,* 1998. Retrieved Oct. 17, 2006, from http://www.emoderators.com/ipct-j/1998/n3-4/hill.html.

4

This chapter covers general guidelines for asking reliable and valid survey questions. Question types and formats also are discussed.

Questions for Online Surveys

The primary function of an evaluation is often to assess the degree of success of a program or to collect information that may be used to improve a program, product, or service. To meet an evaluation's goals and objectives by using an online survey, it is imperative that the questionnaire contain valid and reliable items asked about specific characteristics of the sample. With this in mind, we begin the chapter with a review of some essential guidelines for writing sound survey questions. We then discuss the types of questions found on most evaluation surveys, and finally we consider the variety of question formats available for constructing online surveys.

Guidelines for Writing Survey Questions

To avoid compromising the validity and reliability of your survey responses, it is important to review a few important guidelines for writing good survey questions: evaluators should aim to construct questions that are clear, short, unbiased, and relevant to the target respondents.

Clear Questions. A survey question is clear when the respondents' interpretation of the item matches the surveyor's intended meaning. Moreover, interpretation of the questionnaire items should remain consistent from one respondent to the next. Lack of consistent interpretation across participants results in unreliable responses, a significant threat to the internal validity of the research.

Comprehension difficulties may be caused by the researcher's use of arcane phrases or industry-specific jargon that is unfamiliar to the respondents. These problems are typically uncovered during pretesting, but more insidious are the issues resulting from careless construction of "easy" questions, or lack of specificity through use of everyday language. Consider the question, "Where did you go to school?" By all accounts this is a straightforward item, requiring a simple answer ("Springfield High School," "Pennsylvania," "the University of Pennsylvania"). Although these are all valid answers, the lack of consistency across responses makes data analysis difficult if not impossible. This type of clarity issue can be mitigated by writing the item as a closed-ended question, offering participants a set of response options from which they can select.

Comprehension difficulties noted by Groves and others (2004) may result from the use of common words such as "you" (does this cover the respondent alone or the respondent and his or her family?), "weekend" (is Friday included?), and "children" (defined by age, or by relationship to respondent regardless of age).

Short Questions. In general, shorter questions are better than longer ones. There is seldom a need to write a question that exceeds twenty words. A paragraph-length question on an online survey may be intimidating to some respondents, many of whom will skip the question—or worse, select an answer without reading all of the question text. Consider this one: "Travel to other countries has become increasingly popular recently. Have you ever traveled to another country? If yes, you might have traveled to other countries to enjoy the scenery. How important was the scenery in deciding to take a trip?" Not only is this too long but it also is an example of a double-barreled question, asking about more than one item at a time. The problem can be easily be corrected by rewriting this as two questions: "Have you ever traveled to a foreign country?" "How important was the scenery in your decision to take the trip?"

Unbiased Questions. Biased questions contain words or phrases that lead the respondent to a particular answer. They are also called leading or loaded questions, setting up the respondent to provide the answer the researcher is seeking ("Do you think the new cafeteria provides better food than the old cafeteria?"). An unbiased version of the same question might read, "How do you feel about the variety of food offered by the new cafeteria?" Leading questions usually result in less variance in responses than if the question is asked in an unbiased way.

The only situation wherein it might be acceptable to include a leading question on a survey is to elicit a valid response if you feel participants may not answer honestly, because they are inclined to offer a socially desirable response. If you want to ask about a sensitive issue such as alcoholism, you can include a preface: "Many prominent people have publicly admitted that they have sought help for problems related to alcohol abuse. In the past year, have you been to see a physician or other health care professional because you thought you were drinking too much?" This gives the respondents permission to behave in a socially unacceptable way and lets them know that the behavior you are asking about is not unusual.

Relevant Questions. Not every issue that is of concern to the evaluation team is of interest or concern to the target respondents. Consider the respondents' interest in and ability to answer the questions on the online survey. If they do not have knowledge of a subject, this does not mean they will skip the question; on the contrary, they are likely to respond anyway, particularly if the question asks for an opinion. If you ask students to evaluate government spending on social programs, they may give an opinion despite having little knowledge about the subject. Most people do not want to appear uninformed, so rather than admit to having little or no knowledge about an issue they are likely to select a response option.

Question Type

There are four general categories of questions that might appear on an evaluation survey: (1) factual questions, (2) questions about behavior, (3) attitude questions, and (4) demographic questions. Most questionnaires consist of a variety of these question types. The general guidelines for writing good survey questions apply to all of these categories, but there are some unique considerations associated with each type that should be addressed.

Factual Questions. Factual questions are those that ask respondents to retrieve specific information from their knowledge base and report it to the surveyor ("With which political party are you registered?" "Have you ever had a stroke?"). Unlike attitude questions, factual questions have correct answers. Another form of the factual question resembles a quiz item (typically with true or false presented as response options). In evaluating a health communication campaign, for example, it might be desirable to find out what respondents know about heart-healthy behavior at the start of the campaign so that knowledge gain can be measured at the end of the campaign period.

There is some debate among survey methodologists over including an explicit "don't know" option on a survey questionnaire. Those who prefer not to do so claim it gives lazy respondents a way out of having to think about the question. When writing factual questions, however, it is important to include the choice, because some respondents may simply not know the answer.

Questions About Behavior. Questions about behavior are also knowledge questions. However, they ask about what people *do*, not what they *know*. Unless the research participants have been instructed to keep records of the behavior being studied, most respondents will not be able to furnish accurate estimates of their behavior. Even questions such as "How many miles do you drive in an average week?" or "How much did you spend on prescription drugs last year?" are difficult for many individuals to answer accurately. Asking about specific behavior over a limited and recent time period can help participants focus on a specific instance and aid their recall ("How many miles did you drive yesterday?").

Another approach to improving the accuracy of behavioral estimates is to break the question into subcategories. Instead of asking about "food intake" generally, you might ask how much fish, red meat, chicken, vegetables, and so on, the respondent ate in the past week. This can be easily taken to the extreme by asking questions such as how many orange vegetables the respondent ate last week. If this level of detail is necessary for the evaluation, it is more efficient to give the participants a diary in which to record the behavior being investigated.

Precision of behavioral estimates can be further enhanced by using significant life events (birthdays, marriage, the birth of a child) to aid recall rather than a calendar period (weeks, months, years). For example, "Since your last birthday how many times have you visited your primary care physician?" Respondents know when their last birthday was, but they might not know what you mean if you ask, "In the past year, how many times did you visit your primary care physician?" Does "the past year" mean from a year ago until today or since January 1 of this year?

Attitude Questions. An attitude is a predisposition toward people, places, institutions, and so forth. Underlying attitudes are expressed as opinions on survey questionnaires. Measuring attitude involves asking individuals about their feelings toward something. Attitude is typically measured with a series of items, which can be combined to form an attitude index or scale. Although it is sometimes necessary to write original questions to assess attitude, there are many existing attitude scales from which researchers can choose. These scales have been thoroughly tested and employed by evaluators in a variety of fields. To locate some examples, consult the ERIC Clearinghouse on Assessment and Evaluation (http://www.ericae.net).

The most common attitude question used on evaluation surveys is the Likert-type item. These items present a declarative statement followed by a series of options that ask for the respondent's level of agreement, typically a five-point scale anchored by "strongly agree" on one end and "strongly disagree" on the other. Figure 4.1 illustrates a Likert-type scale. Note that this example includes the "neutral" option in the middle of the responses.

Many researchers prefer to use a four-point scale, eliminating the "neutral" option and thus forcing respondents to either agree or disagree with the statement. Without the middle point, the item better discriminates between positive and neutral, but if respondents are truly neutral about a statement they might become frustrated and skip the question—or perhaps even abandon the survey at this point.

Whether you opt for a four- or five-point scale, consider using scale labels. Some researchers prefer to label just the end points of the scale, that is, only the "strongly agree" and "strongly disagree." Others prefer to label each option, as in Figure 4.1. Labeling each point on the scale helps to improve reliability of measurement, because it leaves less room for individual respondents to assign their own interpretation to the midpoints.

Demographic Questions. Like factual questions, demographic questions also ask respondents to report such details about their background as age, race, income, and so on. This information may be used to address one or more of the research objectives, or it may be used to segment the sample so that subsets (for instance, male and female) can be compared. Additionally,

Figure 4.1. Example of a Likert-Type Scale

I would recommend this program to a friend.

☐ Strongly agree ☐ Agree ☐ Neutral ☐ Disagree ☐ Strongly disagree

demographic information is necessary in data reporting to yield a profile of the survey respondents.

General demographic items are gender, age, level of education, income, marital status, religious affiliation, race or ethnicity, and occupation. Depending on the project objectives, other items such as political party identification, mother's and father's level of education, and number of individuals living in a household may be included. Because some respondents may consider these questions to be sensitive, it is important to ask only for data that are relevant to the research objectives. It may be possible to avoid collecting demographic information by using data already available to you, perhaps data collected during other stages of the evaluation project. For example, if you are surveying high school seniors, it is probably unnecessary to ask about age.

Demographic questions function best when placed at the end of a questionnaire. By the time the respondent nears the end of the questionnaire, he or she has invested some time and effort into answering earlier questions and is more likely to answer these questions than if they appear at the beginning of the questionnaire. In addition, it is a good idea to include a brief preface to the demographic section of the questionnaire, repeating the promise of confidentiality if it was given in the first place.

Response Format

There are two general categories of response formats for survey questions: closed-ended and open-ended questions. Closed-ended questions, such as multiple-choice, rating, ranking, and contingency questions, present a set of response options from which the participants must select. Open-ended questions do not contain response options and rely on the respondent to type an answer into an open text box on the online survey.

Multiple Choice. Similar to multiple-choice questions on exams, this kind of question on an online survey must contain a list of response options that are mutually exclusive. Respondents should not feel they match more than one response category at a time. Options also must be exhaustive, presenting all possible answers that can reasonably be expected (see Figure 4.2). There are several ways to present response options for a multiple-choice question on an online survey, common ones being radio buttons, check boxes, and drop-down menus.

Rating Scales. To capture varying degrees of emotion about a particular topic, it is useful to employ rating questions, such as the Likert-type question discussed earlier. A rating question asks respondents to report the degree to

Figure 4.2. Multiple-Choice Question

What is your highest postbaccalaureate goal?
○ Certificate
○ Master's Degree
○ Specialist
○ Ph.D.
○ Other
[   ]

which they have a feeling about a certain item (see Figure 4.3). Satisfaction and product rating scales are other examples of common scale questions in online surveys used for evaluation.

Ranking. A ranking question requires respondents to indicate, in order, their preference among a list of options (see Figure 4.4). Each item in the list is compared to the others, and no two items can receive the same rank. Generally, ranking questions are discouraged for self-administered surveys, because respondents can mistakenly assign the same rank to more than one option on the list. Online surveys, however, can be programmed such that an error message is generated if the respondent makes a mistake. Unless it is necessary to rank-order a list of alternatives, rating questions are preferable

Figure 4.3. Rating Scale Question

It is important to me to be recognized as an expert in my field.
○ Strongly Agree   ○ Agree   ○ Disagree   ○ Strongly Disagree

Figure 4.4. Ranking Question

Please rank the features that are most important to you when selecting a bank or credit union. One is least important, 5 is most important. Use each rank only once.

	1	2	3	4	5
Location	○	○	○	○	○
Staff	○	○	○	○	○
Services provided	○	○	○	○	○
Low account fees	○	○	○	○	○
ATM locations	○	○	○	○	○

Figure 4.5. Contingency Questions

Have you ever purchased food or beverages at the Panda Express?
○ Yes
○ No

(If the answer to the above question was "yes" respondents would see the screen below).

How satisfied were you with the quality of the food/beverages at the Panda Express?
○ Completely Satisfied   ○ Satisfied   ○ Dissatisfied   ○ Completely Dissatisfied
How satisfied were you with the overall responsiveness of the staff?
○ Completely Satisfied   ○ Satisfied   ○ Dissatisfied   ○ Completely Dissatisfied
How satisfied were you with the cleanliness of the Panda Express?
○ Completely Satisfied   ○ Satisfied   ○ Dissatisfied   ○ Completely Dissatisfied

for many evaluation objectives. The results of a ranking tell you which is the most preferred option, which is the second most preferred, and so forth; ratings allow the respondent to supply feedback about each individual item.

Contingency Questions. A great advantage of online survey administration is the ability to easily ask contingency questions. They also are known as branching or filter questions, because the answer to a particular question determines which subsequent questions the respondents see next. For example, a set of questions about the respondent's health might begin with one about gender. Men and women would then be directed to differing follow-up questions. Contingency questions are also effective for use-of-service and satisfaction items. Respondents might first be asked if they use a service or have visited an establishment; those who respond yes would then be asked to rate their satisfaction with the service or establishment (see Figure 4.5).

Figure 4.6. Open-Ended Question

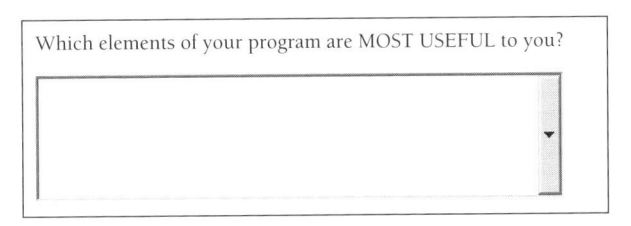

Which elements of your program are MOST USEFUL to you?
[   ]

Open-Ended. Open-ended questions have the potential to collect valid and detailed information, because they allow participants to answer in their own words by typing a response into an open text box (see Figure 4.6). Survey developers tend use open-ended questions sparingly, if at all, on self-administered questionnaires, because they result in more item nonresponse than do closed-ended questions. However, research evidence is starting to show that respondents to online surveys are more likely to answer open-ended questions than are respondents to other self-administered formats (Schaefer and Dillman, 1998). Use of open-ended questions in online surveys seems promising, but at present they should be used judiciously because analysis of these items is more time-consuming than analysis of closed-ended items.

Summary

Good online survey questions are clear, short, unbiased, and relevant to the target respondents. Some combination of factual, behavioral, attitudinal, and demographic questions can be found on most evaluation surveys, and there are a variety of response formats from which to choose in writing these questions. The multiple-choice, rating, and ranking questions used for online administration are similar to the analogous question formats used in other self-administered surveys; online questionnaires are unique, however, in their ability to present complex contingency questions and collect open-ended data more effectively than paper-based questionnaires.

References

Groves, R. M., Fowler, F. J., Couper, M. P., Lepkowski, J. M., Singer, E., and Tourangeau, R. *Survey Methodology*. Hoboken, N.J.: Wiley, 2004.

Schaefer, R., and Dillman, D. A. "Development of a Standard E-mail Methodology: Results of an Experiment." *Public Opinion Quarterly*, 1998, 62(3), 378–397.

5
In this chapter, we describe development of the online survey questionnaire, including organization, layout, formatting, and response formats.

The Survey Questionnaire

Internet-based surveys are still relatively new, and researchers are just beginning to articulate best practices for questionnaire design. Online questionnaire design has generally been guided by the principles applying to other self-administered instruments, such as paper-based questionnaires. Web-based questionnaires, however, have the potential to include pop-up instructions, error messages, and illustrative graphics; they also can use complicated skip patterns that are not possible in other self-administered modes of data collection. These unique capabilities necessitate guidelines specific for the creation of online questionnaires. In this chapter, we draw on the work of Dillman (2000) and Lumsden and Morgan (2005) to present a framework for online questionnaire construction. These guidelines combine the well-established principles of design of paper-based questionnaires with principles of Web page design, especially with respect to usability and accessibility.

Questionnaire Organization

Regardless of length or subject matter, most online questionnaires conform to a general structure. A brief welcome page or message should greet the respondents and motivate them to participate. There may be a need for a login screen requiring participants to use a password to access the survey; instructions for completing the questionnaire will be required. Questions should be presented in a logical and conventional fashion, and a thank-you message acknowledging the respondents' contribution typically concludes the questionnaire.

Welcome. Begin with a welcome message. This may be a separate screen or in the case of a short questionnaire it may be included at the top of the first page. The message should include information about the

Figure 5.1. Welcome Screen Example

Orientation Evaluation Survey

Welcome!

<u>Help</u>   <u>FAQs</u>   <u>Contact Us</u>

Thank you for taking the time to participate in this survey. Your responses are very important to us. This survey gives you an opportunity to voice your opinions and send us feedback about the Fall Orientation. The questionnaire takes about 10 minutes to complete. All of your responses will remain confidential. If you have any questions, feel free to contact us at help@evalsurvey.edu or call us at 555-555-5555.

Click here to begin the survey.

---

sponsoring organization, describe the purpose of the survey, explain how and why the respondent was chosen for participation, discuss the conditions of anonymity and confidentiality, give the estimated time needed to complete the questionnaire, and explain how to redeem incentives if applicable (see Figure 5.1). This also is a good opportunity to encourage completion of the questionnaire by emphasizing the importance of each individual's participation. Welcome messages should be brief and simple, avoiding use of animation or other Web effects that may cause the page to load slowly.

Login Screen. A login screen is necessary if you wish to restrict access to the questionnaire (see Figure 5.2). This is particularly important when using a randomly selected sample from the population of interest. With a

Figure 5.2. Login Screen Example

Orientation Evaluation Survey

Please enter your four-digit password in the box below.

[   ]

Continue

random sample, it is essential that only selected respondents participate; uninvited participants should not be permitted to answer survey questions. Passwords can be assigned to participants and included in the e-mail invitation to take part in the survey. To prevent errors, avoid using dashes or spaces in passwords, and keep them as short and simple as possible.

Instructions. Directions for completing the questionnaire may be included on the welcome page or at the top of the first page of questions. They should be general instructions about how to progress through the questionnaire; for particular information regarding specific questions, use links or pop-up windows near the location of those items on the questionnaire.

Questions. With respect to questions and how they are presented in an online questionnaire, we can rely on generally accepted standards for paper-based questionnaires. There are a number of specific issues to consider in using online surveys, notably questionnaire length, question order, and treatment of sensitive questions.

Questionnaire Length. There is little agreement about the optimal length of a questionnaire. In general, a shorter questionnaire elicits greater response and results in less abandonment than a longer one. This issue may be of particular concern in using online surveys because people's eyes become fatigued faster reading a computer screen than words on paper. If surveying a specific population, such as an employee group or individuals participating in an experimental program, the questionnaire may be longer, because the people in the sample have a vested interest in participating. In determining ideal length, consider the time it takes an average respondent to complete the questionnaire rather than the number of questions included. It may be the case that a questionnaire containing fifty questions can be completed in ten minutes and one with twenty-five questions may take an hour; variations in the nature and format of the questions result in differing completion times.

Question Order. The first questions should be easy to answer and require no more than a few seconds for respondents to decide. These initial questions set the tone for the remainder of the questionnaire and can either encourage respondents to continue or cause them to drop out. Group similar questions together, whether by topic or response format. It is best to begin with closed-ended questions and then move to open-ended ones. An exception to this is if you are asking open- and closed-ended questions about the same topic. In this case, begin with the open-ended items to prevent influencing respondents with the options of the closed-ended questions. Place demographic items toward the end (unless they are to be used as filter questions), because many respondents find these questions to be sensitive and may be reluctant to answer them.

Sensitive Questions. Personal, delicate, or tricky questions should appear near the middle or at the two-thirds point of the questionnaire. By this time, respondents are warmed up and have invested some time and effort in completing the survey, so they are more likely to answer the sensitive questions.

Thank You. The last screen, or last section, of the questionnaire should be reserved for a thank-you statement. Other information on this page may be an e-mail address for respondents to provide feedback or comments and an address or phone number for contacting the institutional review board that approved the research. You also may want to inform respondents about how to access the results of the survey.

Layout

As with any self-administered questionnaire, an online questionnaire needs to create a positive visual impression. The questions and their associated response options should be presented in an easy-to-read, uncluttered manner. There should be enough space between questions to avoid confusion, and questions should never be separated from their response sets. Unless you have a specific reason for doing so (such as including a screening question), do not require respondents to answer one question before moving on to the next. This can be frustrating for respondents and is considered by many survey methodologists to be unethical, because answering any item on a questionnaire should be voluntary.

There is some controversy over whether to develop single-page questionnaires that require respondents to scroll down to answer all of the questions or to create a multipage, nonscrolling questionnaire. On the one hand, excessive scrolling can be annoying and cause dropout; on the other hand, too much clicking on navigation buttons can cause frustration and become discouraging. The overall length of the questionnaire can serve as a guide for which option to choose. For a short questionnaire, use the single-page scrolling format, and multipage formatting for a longer one. If a questionnaire is to contain skip logic, then the multipage format is necessary.

Navigation

To help respondents navigate through longer online questionnaires, developers can incorporate a variety of devices, including buttons, progress bars, and links. Whichever options you choose, all navigation guides should be clearly identified, be consistent in color and size, and appear in the same location on all questionnaire pages.

Buttons. Navigation buttons allow respondents to move backward and forward within the questionnaire. They should be used sparingly and be large enough so that respondents with visual impairment can spot them (see Figure 5.3).

Figure 5.3. Navigation Buttons

| Clear | Back | Next |

Figure 5.4. Progress Bar

| Progress | | 50% |

Progress Bars. One way to let respondents know where they are in the questionnaire is to include a progress bar (see Figure 5.4). Although some developers choose not to use progress bars for longer questionnaires for fear of alienating respondents, it is not an advisable practice to forgo them. Most respondents appreciate knowing how much of the questionnaire remains to be completed.

Links. Links are common on Web sites, and respondents with Web experience will be familiar with them. They can be useful for offering definition of terms or to connect to a source external to the questionnaire. Be sure that links are clearly and descriptively labeled (for example, use blue, bold, or underlined text, as is the custom in Web design), and indicate that a link has been visited by changing its color. If your target population is older (with difficulty differentiating between blue and black) or is primarily male (males are more likely to be color blind), you may want to avoid using the blue color to distinguish links, because they may not easily recognize the color change. It is best to exercise restraint in including links on questionnaires even if your sample is Web-savvy because exploring them lengthens the time it takes to complete the questionnaire.

Formatting

There are several formatting issues to be considered in designing Web-based questionnaires: the appearance of text, color, graphics, and animation.

Text. The fonts used for online questionnaires should be familiar and, most important, easy to read on the screen. Arial and Times New Roman are two common choices with which most respondents will be familiar. A 12-point type will be serviceable for the general population; a 14-point type is preferable for users with disabilities or the elderly. If applicable, ensure that the text can be read by screen readers in a logical order. Consider as well the order in which visually impaired users will hear the elements of a question, including the instructions and response options. Finally, use bold characters or all capital letters to emphasize text, rather than italics, which can be difficult to read on a computer screen. A font called *Read Regular* can be helpful to people with dyslexia, because the characters are distinct.

Color. Colors can have considerable impact on an online questionnaire; they can create mood (good and bad) and have a host of cultural and social associations. Color selection should be made with the target audience demographics in mind. Too many colors can be distracting; a neutral background such as white or off-white with black text is usually a safe choice. In general, colors of high contrast ensure maximum readability. Be cautious of color combinations that may cause visual vibrations and after-images, or those that may not be discernible to color-blind respondents, specifically red and green, yellow and blue, blue and red, and blue and green. Additionally, the triple combination of blue, yellow, and green can be difficult for some senior citizens to discriminate.

Graphics. Use graphics sparingly. They can increase download time and possibly decrease the accessibility of the questionnaire among some users. Showing a large graphic at a small size on a Web page does not reduce the time needed to download the image. Individual images should be around 5kb in size, and individual Web pages should be limited to about 20kb of graphics in total. If you know that your sample will access the questionnaire via a high-speed connection, then you can use more graphics and perhaps audio or video content, if relevant to your survey. If graphics are used, it is important to provide ALT tags containing descriptive text about the image for respondents with visual impairment.

Animation. Although it may be tempting to include Flash animation on your online questionnaire, it is generally not advisable, because it requires certain browser versions or plug-ins. Flash also can be problematic for respondents who use assistive technology. If you do choose to go this route, offering the option to view a static form of the questionnaire ensures that all potential respondents are able to participate.

Response Formats

Developers have a choice of several technical mechanisms to facilitate responses to closed- and open-ended survey questions. The options include radio buttons, check boxes, drop-down menus, matrix questions, and open-text boxes.

Radio Buttons. A radio button is a small circle with text next to it (see Figure 5.5). When the respondent clicks on the circle, it is filled in with a smaller, solid circle or a check mark. Radio buttons are traditionally used if the respondent must select exactly one response from the set provided. They are popular because they resemble paper-based questionnaire answer formats. However, radio buttons can be frustrating for inexperienced Web

Figure 5.5. Radio Buttons

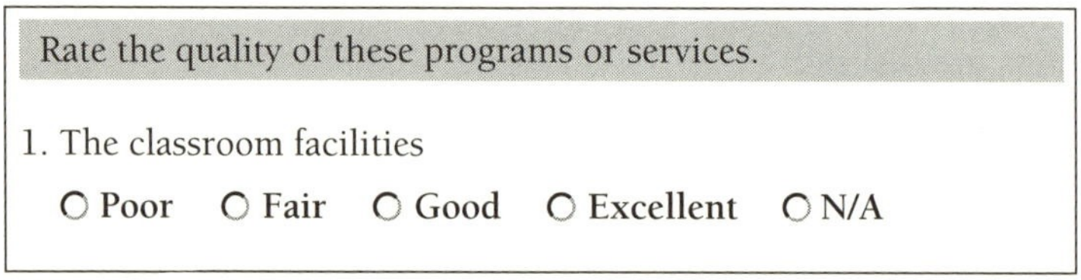

Rate the quality of these programs or services.

1. The classroom facilities
   ○ Poor   ○ Fair   ○ Good   ○ Excellent   ○ N/A

users, because they require a certain level of precision. Sufficient spacing surrounding each button assists users with motor impairment.

Check Boxes. A check box is a small box with text next to it. Clicking on a box places a check mark in that box. They are typically used when respondents are permitted to select "all that apply" from the list of options. See Figure 5.6 for an example of a multiple-choice question that uses a check-box format for response options. Like radio buttons, they also demand a certain degree of mouse precision; spacing surround response options presented with checkboxes should therefore be sufficient such that clicking on one box does not accidentally select a nearby box.

Drop-Down Menus. A drop-down menu has a window and contents (response options) that become visible when the respondent clicks the title or small arrow next to the title (see Figure 5.7). Drop-down menus should be reserved for questions that have a lengthy list of response options, as with

Figure 5.6. Check Boxes

Why did you decide to take this online course? (Check all that apply.)

☐ Lack of available on-ground course
☐ Prefer online courses
☐ Student recommended
☐ Professor recommended
☐ Other _____

Figure 5.7. Drop-Down Menu

What is your country of citizenship?

United States ▼

United States
US Minor Outlying Islands
Uruguay
Uzbekistan
Vanuatu
Vatican City State
Venezuela
Viet Nam
Virgin Islands (British)
Virgin Islands (U.S.)
Wallis/Futuna Islands

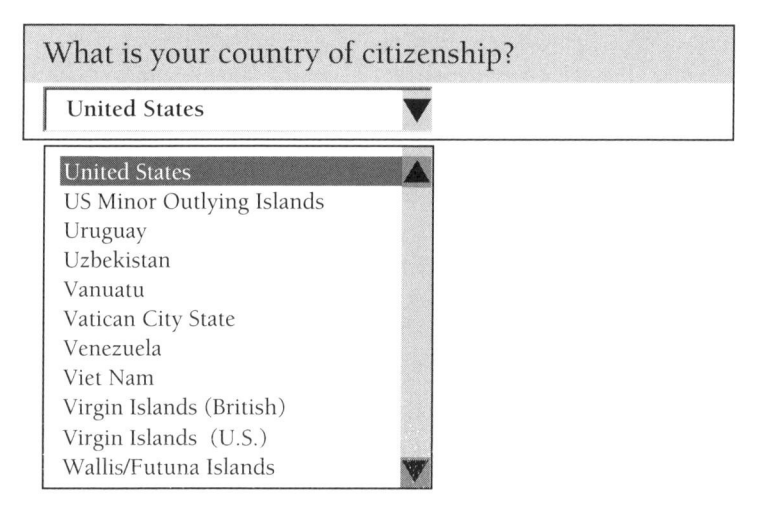

zip codes in several counties. If a drop-down menu is used, it is important that a default option not be visible, because this can lead some respondents to believe that the question has already been answered. Either leave the visible window blank or include an instruction such as "click here" or "enter response."

Matrix Questions. Matrix formats condense a series of questions into one list, typically using an attitude or some other sort of rating scale. They are a convenient way to collect multiple responses regarding one topic and generally can be answered quickly, because respondents read one statement and then select scale responses as they relate to a number of characteristics (see Figure 5.8).

Open-Text Boxes. An open- or free-text box has a space for respondents to type in their answer to an open-ended question (see Figure 5.9). The boxes may be short enough to accommodate one or two words or longer for essay-type answers. The size of the text box should be considered carefully, because respondents take their cue about how much to write on the basis of the size of the text box.

Pretesting the Questionnaire

The final step in designing the online questionnaire is to test it with a small sample of your target respondents. These pretest respondents can offer feedback about the usefulness of instructions, clarity of questions, technical performance of the questionnaire, and the length of time to complete it. If you receive substantial feedback from the pretest respondents, then it may

Figure 5.8. Matrix Question

Thinking about your graduate experience so far, to what extent do you feel that you have made progress in each of the following areas?

	Very little	Some	Quite a bit	Very much
Developing in-depth knowledge in your discipline	☐	☐	☐	☐
Developing research skills	☐	☐	☐	☐
Developing advanced writing skills	☐	☐	☐	☐
Developing the ability to work well in groups	☐	☐	☐	☐
Developing competencies needed for your career	☐	☐	☐	☐
Developing a professional network	☐	☐	☐	☐

Figure 5.9. Open-Text Box

What is the name of the city or town where you live?

be necessary to conduct a second pretest after revisions have been made to the questionnaire.

Summary

This chapter has outlined a set of general guidelines for designing online questionnaires. These guidelines are based on principles developed for creation of paper-based questionnaires and on general Web page design strategies. As the Internet becomes more diffused into society and Web technology, including software for designing online surveys, advances, these principles will require updating.

References

Dillman, D. A. *Mail and Internet Surveys: The Tailored Design Method.* Hoboken, N.J.: Wiley, 2000.

Lumsden, J., and Morgan, W. "Online-Questionnaire Design: Establishing Guidelines and Evaluating Existing Support." In *Proceedings of Sixteenth International Conference of the Information Resources Management Association,* May 15–18, 2005.

6

In this chapter, we explore fielding an online survey, recruiting subjects, and increasing the response rate.

Conducting the Survey

Research regarding the optimal fielding of online surveys is in its infancy and just beginning to offer clear suggestions for effective recruiting of participants as well as techniques for maximizing the response rate. In this chapter, we discuss the process of recruiting participants by e-mailing invitations to a list of recipients selected from a sampling frame and by posting the survey to a Web site and advertising its presence. We also review how standard techniques for increasing survey response rate can be applied to online surveys.

Recruiting Participants

After you have created your online survey, recruit your sample. The three primary ways to recruit participants for an online survey are sending e-mail invitations to members of a sampling frame, creating a Web presence, and posting an invitation to a listserv or newsgroup.

E-mail Invitations. An e-mail invitation is a short message, usually three or fewer paragraphs long, announcing the survey and providing a link to the Web site containing the questionnaire. The invitation should emphasize the ease and importance of responding; offer instructions about how to proceed; and passwords, if applicable. Incentives, if made available, also should be mentioned in the e-mail invitation.

If you selected your sample from a sampling frame, then most likely you have a list of e-mail addresses of the potential respondents. In this case, the list can be imported into the Web survey host's address book and you can e-mail an invitation to each potential participant. For example, a large California university wanted to evaluate the effectiveness of their new student services hub. The university randomly sampled two thousand students from a sampling frame of fourteen thousand who were enrolled for the fall quarter. Each selected student received an e-mail invitation to participate in the survey.

Creating a Web Presence. If you do not have a list of e-mail addresses of potential respondents, you will employ alternative methods for recruiting respondents. Posting a survey on a Web site is one option. The mere presence of a survey on a Web page, however, is unlikely to attract respondents; the survey must be advertised. One frequently used technique is to use pop-up messages to announce the survey. This approach depends on visitors noticing the advertisement and becoming intrigued enough to click through to complete the survey. Many individuals, however, feel that pop-up messages are invasive and have taken steps to block such uninvited intrusions.

Listservs and Newsgroups. Posting a survey invitation to a listserv or newsgroup is another method of recruitment for online surveys. This technique is useful for contacting rare or difficult-to-reach populations. For example, a researcher studying illicit drug dealers posted a survey invitation to twenty-three English-language drug-related newsgroups and received eighty responses. There are some obvious disadvantages with this approach. Individuals who are not part of the population of interest may belong to the listserv and respond to the survey, and the invitation may be forwarded to other newsgroups, such that the researcher does not know how many people received the invitation and cannot compute a response rate.

Sending thousands of e-mail messages to members of a listserv may lead to the perception that you are posting junk mail. There are some steps to alleviate this problem. First, contact the moderator of the list to inquire about the appropriateness of your request and to get permission to contact the members; next, e-mail individual groups separately, because e-mailing several groups at once will give the appearance that you are spamming them; and finally, explain to the recipients that your survey is not an advertisement in disguise, furnish some information about the research, and supply the contact e-mail address or phone number of the sponsoring organization.

Increasing Response Rate

Perhaps one of the most challenging tasks in conducting an online survey is to obtain a sufficient response rate. Recipients of e-mail invitations can easily delete your message from their e-mail inbox, and it is difficult to attract the attention of visitors to Web sites. In working with an e-mail list of potential respondents, sending a follow-up invitation can help increase the response rate. Individuals who are interested in completing the survey but put it off until a later date are reminded and likely to follow through with their intended participation. Research evidence indicates that a follow-up message sent approximately one week after the initial e-mail invitation is optimal; the additional increase in response rate yielded by a second and third follow-up is negligible (Kittleson, 1997).

Most online survey software vendors offer a list management function that allows researchers to sort the list by completion; this way, only those respondents who have not yet responded are contacted with the reminder message.

In addition to follow-up messages, incentives and application of behavioral theory also can serve to increase the response rate for an online survey.

Incentives. The use of incentives is a heavily researched area in the response-rate literature. Although the technique is not specific to online survey research, the bulk of the research suggests that incentives are effective in increasing the response rate in other survey settings. The data also suggest that there is some merit in offering a chance at one large incentive (a prize drawing) rather than the promise of a smaller incentive. This issue is far from settled, however.

The most common incentive for participating in an online survey is money, perhaps $20 for each respondent, or a chance at a drawing for a larger sum. If you have a sampling frame, it is possible to calculate how much you can afford to spend on incentives for each individual participant. If, however, you are recruiting respondents from Web sites or listservs, it is not possible to predict how many respondents you will get and therefore cannot promise a particular sum of money. Keep in mind that in both cases you must record the e-mail address of respondents so that they can be instructed about how to receive their incentive.

Behavioral Theory. If potential respondents follow the norm of social responsibility, then they are likely to comply with a request if it is presented in terms of asking for help. For example, in your e-mail invitation you might say "your participation would really help us out." In this situation, you depend on respondents' desire to view themselves as helpful and generous people.

Salience is how important or relevant a topic is to the potential respondent. Survey salience may not be within your control, because the project goals dictate the questionnaire content; nevertheless, it is useful to consider the issue in designing questionnaires and invitations. The more relevant the topic seems, the more likely a respondent is to participate. If appropriate, you might point out that the recipient has been contacted because of his or her past action (such as attending a workshop); that his or her participation has implications for a system or process (for example, "Your suggestions will help us to improve our service"); or that the respondent will benefit tangibly ("Your feedback will determine how we structure your division").

Summary

Online survey research methodology is still a new and rapidly developing field. Accordingly, research evidence on which we can base recommendations for best practices regarding the fielding of electronic surveys is emerging. Evaluators working with closed populations for which there are readily available sampling frames may use e-mail invitations to contact potential respondents for participation in a survey. The lack of such a list necessitates other strategies, such as posting the survey on a Web site and using advertisements to entice participation, or inviting subscribers to a listserv or newsgroup to participate.

Although much of the evidence about the effectiveness of incentives for increasing the response rate in a Web survey has not been fully vetted, some recommendations can be suggested. It is advisable to offer some incentive rather than no incentive. A chance to win a substantial sum in a lottery drawing is more attractive than the guarantee of a small amount of money. Finally, relying on individuals' desire to view themselves as helpful people, and increasing the salience of the survey topic to the potential respondents, may also help to increase the response rate in an online survey.

Reference

Kittleson, M. "Determining Effective Follow-up of E-mail Surveys." *American Journal of Health Behavior*, 1997, 21(3), 193–196.

In this chapter we discuss how to download, clean, and transform online survey results in preparation for data analysis.

Managing Online Survey Data

Managing data collected from online surveys may be a straightforward process involving no more than downloading a spreadsheet from a Web survey host and presenting descriptive statistics associated with each questionnaire item. On the other hand, if the evaluation objectives require more complex analysis and presentation of the data, it will be necessary to investigate your Web host's capability for either conducting advanced analyses online or exporting the data to another software program for more sophisticated analysis. In this chapter, we explore the fundamentals of managing online survey results, including downloading and cleaning data and transforming data.

Downloading and Cleaning Data

Many popular Web survey hosts allow users to view results on their Web site in real time. That is, as the questionnaires are completed data summaries are automatically updated. The typical display includes frequency (the number of respondents selecting each response option) and an associated percentage. Bar charts are the usual mode of presentation, and some ASPs (application service providers) have options for other formats such as a histogram or pie chart. (Figure 7.1 is an example of SurveyMonkey's basic results report.) Also common among most Web hosts is the ability to share results with respondents or with other interested parties.

Some evaluators find that the descriptive data summaries available on the host's Web site are insufficient for their reporting needs. For example, you may want to compare two or more groups of respondents and conduct a statistical test to determine if there are differences among them. In this

52   USING ONLINE SURVEYS IN EVALUATION

Figure 7.1. SurveyMonkey's Basic Results Report

Results Summary

2. Site Use

1. How did you first learn about SurveyMonkey?

	Response Percent	Response Total
Took someone else's survey	34%	11315
Banner Advertisement	5.5%	1816
Search Engine	14.7%	4901
Referral/Link from another site	16.1%	5375
Magazine/Print Advertisement	5.9%	1955
Other (please specify)	23.9%	7957
Total Respondents		33319
(skipped this question)		12

3. Demographic

2. What kind of connection do you have to the Internet?

	Response Percent	Response Total
28.8 Kbps modem	2.6%	693
56 Kbps modem	6.2%	1649
ISDN	6.7%	1807
Cable modem	19.9%	5336
DSL	24.7%	6620
T1 or better	19%	5078
Do not know	20.9%	5602
Total Respondents		26785
(skipped this question)		6577

3. Where are you located?

	Response Percent	Response Total
United States	72.5%	18679
Other Country	27.5%	7097
Total Respondents		25776
(skipped this question)		7551

4. Future Directions (continued)

4. Are you satisfied with the overall usability of SurveyMonkey? If not, tell us how we can improve...

	Response Percent	Response Total
Haven't used it yet	65.4%	14952
Yes	31.3%	7151
No	3.4%	771
Total Respondents		22874
(skipped this question)		10450

5. What other features would you like to see added to SurveyMonkey?

Total Respondents		4399
(skipped this question)		28926

5. Future Directions

6. The following features may be added to SurveyMonkey in the near future. Please rate the importance of the following features.

	Very Important	Important	Somewhat Important	Not Important	Response Total
Survey templates	56% (10114)	32% (5794)	9% (1706)	3% (583)	18197
Increased multi-lingual support	22% (3895)	29% (4969)	25% (4277)	24% (4180)	17321
Multiple Users per Account	33% (5762)	35% (6171)	22% (3802)	10% (1699)	17434
Graphical charts of response data	51% (9076)	32% (5754)	11% (1994)	5% (976)	17800
Increased Export Functionality	47% (8181)	34% (5910)	13% (2269)	6% (1113)	17473
Total Respondents					18973
(skipped this question)					14352

NEW DIRECTIONS FOR EVALUATION • DOI: 10.1002/ev

case, the options are to choose an inclusive software program that has the capability for advanced statistical analyses or else download your results (typically in Excel format) so that the data can then be imported into a data analysis program such as SPSS, SAS, or Minitab. It is preferable for the host to offer the option to download data directly in one of these file formats. Follow the downloading instructions furnished by the particular survey host or software.

Once downloaded, the data file must be cleaned before analyses can be conducted. Begin data cleaning by screening the data file for patterns of missing data, inconsistencies in data, strange patterns in distributions, and extreme values. An easy way to identify any oddities in the data is to create frequency distribution tables and graphs for each questionnaire item.

If any strange values exist, determine the source of the problem and make the necessary corrections. Impossible values are the easiest to correct. For example, if someone types in an open-text box that he or she is two years old (and you did not survey two-year-olds), you can safely assume that this was a mistake (perhaps the respondent meant to type twenty) and code it as a missing value. Values that are possible but improbable—such as someone reporting that he watched fifteen hours of television yesterday—are more challenging. There are a few options. Some statisticians maintain that extreme values should always remain in the data file unchanged; others suggest treatment such as replacing the value with the group mean for that variable; and some allow deletion of the extreme value so long as its exclusion is noted in the final report. These options should be considered within the context of affording the most accurate and ethical data reporting possible.

Transforming Data

After the data file has been cleaned of impossible and improbable values, it may be necessary to transform some of the raw data so that they are usable for analysis. The spreadsheet you download from the Web survey host will be arranged in rows (each row representing one respondent) and columns (each column representing one survey question; see Figure 7.2).

Figure 7.3 is an illustration of one survey question and the codes assigned to the response options when the data were downloaded. Notice that "strongly agree" is coded 1, "agree" is 2, "disagree" is 3, "strongly disagree" is 4, and "n/a" is 5. If you were to compute a mean or any other summary statistic such as a median, mode, or standard deviation, the value 5 would be included in the computation. For this question, we interpret higher mean values as indicating greater disagreement with the statement; by including 5 in the computation we artificially exaggerate the amount of disagreement with the questionnaire item. In this case, the fives should be recoded as missing values and omitted from calculation of summary statistics for the variable.

Figure 7.2. Data Spreadsheet from a Web Survey Host

A	B	C	D	E	F	G	H
ID_#	VERSION	Q1	Q2	Q3	Q4	Q5	Q6
1	A	4	5	2	1	5	2
2	A	4	4	3	2	5	4
3	A	5	4	2	2	3	4
4	A	4	5	3	2	4	3
5	A	5	2	3	3	3	4
6	A	3	1	1	2	5	4
7	A	2	4	3	3	5	2
8	A	5	5	3	3	5	4
9	A	2	4	4	1	5	3
10	A	5	3	3	4	5	4
11	A	5	2	1	2	2	3
12	A	3	2	1	4	5	3
13	A	5	3	2	1	5	5
14	A	1	4	2	5	5	1
15	A	5	4	2	2	5	4
16	A	4	3	3	3	5	4
17	A	4	3	1	2	1	5
18	A	4	1	1	2	5	3
19	A	2	3	1	1	5	4
20	A	5	4	3	3	4	3
21	A	1	1	3	1	3	5
22	A	5	2	3	1	4	2
23	A	3	2	5	3	5	1
24	A	3	4	5	3	5	2
25	A	3	2	1	3	2	97
26	A	2	2	5	1	5	3
27	A	5	4	3	4	5	3
28	A	2	2	1	2	5	3

Figure 7.3. Survey Question with Numerical Code

I am interested in flexible degree requirements.

○ Strongly Agree   ○ Agree   ○ Disagree   ○ Strongly Disagree   ○ N/A
1   2   3   4   5

One other way in which you may want to recode the responses to this question is to flip the scale. That is, change 1 to 4, 2 to 3, 3 to 2, and 4 to 1. There are two possible reasons for doing this: (1) to remain consistent with other scales that may be coded this way, and (2) to facilitate writing the report it may be easier to explain that higher values indicate greater agreement than the other way around.

Two final types of data transformation that may be necessary are arithmetical calculations, as in asking respondents to report their date of birth rather than age (applying a formula for subtracting the respondent's date of birth from the current year will be required) and recoding open-ended questions into categories. For example, if you ask respondents to write in what they felt the most useful features of a course were, you might place those open-ended responses into categories such as "instructor factors," "course materials," "experiential exercises," and so forth, before proceeding with the analysis.

Summary

Although treatment of online survey data may require no more than presenting the descriptive statistics provided by your Web survey host, in some situations it is likely that evaluators charged with investigating complex programs or services will have to download the survey data and apply more complex statistical tools than are available online. Downloaded data must be cleaned and often transformed in some way before analysis can begin. Data cleaning requires investigators to seek out impossible or extreme values in the data set and make decisions about their disposition; data transformation strategies help surveyors format the data for maximum usability.

8

This chapter presents two case studies using online surveys for evaluation: a university needs assessment survey and the follow-up survey; and a four-year, multimillion-dollar statewide evaluation project.

Case Studies

Having discussed creation and implementation of online surveys for evaluation projects, we turn our attention to some case studies presented to illustrate the concepts covered in this volume. We begin with an example of a needs-assessment survey designed to measure the amount of help new students at a university require in their first year. We then discuss the follow-up survey conducted by the same university to measure the effectiveness of the programs implemented on the basis of the needs assessment survey.

To demonstrate how online surveys can be successfully integrated into a large-scale evaluation, we next describe a four-year, multimillion-dollar evaluation of a telemedicine project that used online surveys for needs assessments, process, outcome, and impact evaluation.

A University Needs Assessment Survey—Formative Evaluation

A major U.S. university wanted to improve its student services, thereby increasing student performance and morale and decreasing attrition, particularly among first-time freshmen. To assess the needs of new students, the Office of Institutional Research (OIR) at the university decided to administer an online survey to entering freshmen. The survey was titled "Entering Student Needs Assessment Survey." (Figures 8.1, 8.2, and 8.3 are screens from the online needs assessment survey.) The purpose of the survey was to determine the amount of help the new students would require in specific areas.

Each new student at the university is assigned an e-mail account, and the list of e-mail addresses is maintained by the OIR. The students were told

Figure 8.1. Entering Student Needs Assessment Survey, Page 1

Entering Student Needs Assessment Survey   Exit this survey >>

As you begin your studies, we would like your assessment of the areas in which you hope to make significant gains while at the University. The information you provide will assist us in designing and enhancing programs and services for the student body.

1. On a scale of 1 to 5 where 1 indicates "none at all" and 5 indicates "a great deal" how much help would you say you need in

	1	2	3	4	5	N/A
Clarifying academic goals	☐	☐	☐	☐	☐	☐
Identifying career objectives	☐	☐	☐	☐	☐	☐
Identifying internship opportunities	☐	☐	☐	☐	☐	☐
Acquiring skills to prepare for graduate school	☐	☐	☐	☐	☐	☐

Next >>

Figure 8.2. Entering Student Needs Assessment Survey, Page 2

Entering Student Needs Assessment Survey   Exit this survey >>

2. On a scale of 1 to 5 where 1 indicates "none at all" and 5 indicates "a great deal" how much help would you say you need in

	1	2	3	4	5	N/A
Writing more clearly	☐	☐	☐	☐	☐	☐
Strengthening quantitative skills	☐	☐	☐	☐	☐	☐
Understanding the scientific method	☐	☐	☐	☐	☐	☐
Thinking analytically	☐	☐	☐	☐	☐	☐
Improving study habits	☐	☐	☐	☐	☐	☐
Budgeting time more efficiently	☐	☐	☐	☐	☐	☐
Using the computer as a learning tool	☐	☐	☐	☐	☐	☐
Improving library research skills	☐	☐	☐	☐	☐	☐
Working effectively in groups	☐	☐	☐	☐	☐	☐
Developing leadership skills	☐	☐	☐	☐	☐	☐
Working independently	☐	☐	☐	☐	☐	☐
Understanding science and technology	☐	☐	☐	☐	☐	☐
Integrating concepts from different disciplines	☐	☐	☐	☐	☐	☐
Obtaining a multi-disciplinary education	☐	☐	☐	☐	☐	☐

<< Prev   Next >>

Figure 8.3. Entering Student Needs Assessment Survey, Page 3

Entering Student Needs Assessment Survey   Exit this survey >>

3. On a scale of 1 to 5 where 1 indicates "none at all" and 5 indicates "a great deal" how much help would you say you need in

	1	2	3	4	5	N/A
Speaking more confidently in front of people	☐	☐	☐	☐	☐	☐
Understanding a diverse population	☐	☐	☐	☐	☐	☐
Gaining a broader understanding of other cultures	☐	☐	☐	☐	☐	☐
Expanding the literary works read	☐	☐	☐	☐	☐	☐
Gaining appreciation for current events	☐	☐	☐	☐	☐	☐
Taking advantage of cultural opportunities	☐	☐	☐	☐	☐	☐
Developing appreciation for art	☐	☐	☐	☐	☐	☐
Developing own philosophy of life	☐	☐	☐	☐	☐	☐
Improving physical health	☐	☐	☐	☐	☐	☐

<< Prev   Next >>

about the survey at freshman orientation and encouraged to participate. Entry into a raffle for a $100 gift certificate to the campus bookstore was offered as an incentive to respond to the survey. The survey was created using the services of a Web survey host, and the link was e-mailed in an invitation to all first-time freshmen at the beginning of orientation week; they were given until the end of the week to complete the survey.

The survey results were downloaded from the Web survey host's site and transferred into a statistical software package for analysis. A total of 720 first time freshmen participated in the survey. This represents a 21 percent response rate. Comparison of the survey respondents to the actual population of entering freshmen showed that the ethnic distribution of the sample was comparable; however, females were overrepresented in the sample. Survey respondents also had higher Scholastic Aptitude Test (SAT) scores than the actual population.

More than half the respondents reported they needed a moderate amount of help in three areas: acquiring the knowledge and skills for graduate school, identifying internship opportunities, and expanding the volume and range of literary works read. Additionally, about half the respondents said they needed a moderate amount of help to make gains in understanding science and technology. Table 8.1 is an example of one of the summary tables included in the survey report. The table highlights the ten specific academic and personal skill areas with the highest mean scores, indicating that the students said they needed the most help in these areas.

The survey report was prepared by OIR staff, presented to the relevant university administrators and student service providers, and posted on the university Web site. From the results of the survey, the university's Career Development Center developed a series of workshops designed to help new students focus their career goals, find internships, and identify graduate schools and programs in their interest areas. Additionally, the Student Center for Academic Achievement began offering tutoring in

Table 8.1. Academic and Personal Skill Areas with the Highest Mean Scores

Academic and Personal Skill Area	Total N	Mean Score[a]
Acquire skills to prepare for graduate school	715	3.8
Expand the volume & range of literary works read	719	3.6
Identify internship opportunities	719	3.6
Understand science and technology	718	3.6
Identify career objectives	719	3.5
Integrate concepts from different disciplines	720	3.5
Strengthen quantitative skills	719	3.5
Improve study habits	720	3.4
Gain broader understanding of other cultures	714	3.3
Gain appreciation of current events	719	3.2

[a]Based on a 5-point scale; 1 indicates no help needed, 5 indicates a lot of help needed.

quantitative skills and a Great Works in Literature lecture series. Table 8.2 is an outline of the major processes in this project.

The Entering-Student Needs Assessment Survey was considered a success and will continue to be administered at the beginning of every academic year so that changes in student needs over time may be tracked.

Follow-up to the University Needs Assessment Survey—Summative Evaluation

Pleased with the quality of information collected during the fall Student Needs Assessment Survey, the university decided to conduct a follow-up survey at the end of the school year to determine to what extent the university met the academic, personal, and social needs of the new students.

Table 8.2. Needs Assessment Survey Outline

Entering Student Needs Assessment Survey

Evaluation Goal	• To assess the amount of help new students will need in a variety of areas.
Objectives	• To determine the amount of help entering freshmen believe they need in the following areas: • Academic skills • Career planning • Personal counseling • Social abilities • Cultural awareness
Relevant Stakeholders	• University administrators, student services providers, parents of entering students.
Target Population	• All first-time freshmen entering the University in the current academic year.
Sampling Strategy Sampling frame	• Saturation sampling. • List of e-mail addresses maintained by OIR.
Survey Method	• Web-based survey using host's software and Web hosting of survey.
Timeline	• Survey introduction and initial e-mail distribution on Monday of orientation week; follow-up reminder e-mail on Wednesday of orientation week; survey closes on Friday of orientation week.
	• Descriptive statistics only to be presented in final report.
Data Analysis Plan Reporting	• Survey report distributed to administrators and student services providers.
Application	• Determine the academic, career, personal, social, and cultural awareness programs and services to be created and/or revised. Create and/or revise programs and services as needed.

The follow-up survey was administered to the 720 students who responded to the fall survey. The same Web survey host was used, and a questionnaire that closely resembled the fall survey was constructed. This time, however, instead of asking about areas the students needed to improve, the questions asked the participants to use a five-point scale to indicate the level to which they felt their needs had been met during the academic year. The students were e-mailed an invitation, which included a link to the survey (Figure 8.4 shows the e-mail invitation to participate in the follow-up survey). A total of 164 usable surveys were completed.

Three areas stood out in the fall survey: needing help in acquiring knowledge and skills for graduate school (more than half the respondents), identifying internship opportunities, and expanding the volume and range of literary works read. The follow-up survey gave evidence that the university was successful in helping students meet their goals. For example, 45 percent of the respondents said that the need for acquiring knowledge and skills for graduate school had been at least partially met. Moreover, 43 percent said the same for identifying internship opportunities, and 73 percent indicated similar outcomes on the goal of expanding the volume and range of literary works read.

Although 164 respondents represent only about 5 percent of the entering freshman class at this university, OIR staff were satisfied with the results and plan to survey this cohort again when they complete their sophomore year.

Telemedicine Project

The organization being evaluated (we refer to it as ABC) had an overarching goal to deliver health care services and educational opportunities to rural regions of the state using technology. To help achieve this goal, ABC funded ten grantees throughout the state to provide telemedicine and

Figure 8.4. Needs Assessment Survey Follow-up E-mail Invitation

Dear Student,

This past fall, as an entering freshman, you participated in a needs assessment survey where you indicated areas in which you felt you needed help while at the university. As you complete your first year, we would like to know to what extent your needs have been met. The information you provide will assist us in designing and enhancing programs and services for the student body.

The questionnaire takes about ten minutes to complete. To participate in the survey, click on this link: [www.xxxxxxxx.edu].

Use this password to identify yourself as an eligible participant: [password].

If you have any questions or need help, feel free to call the Office of Institutional Research at (555) 555-5555.

Thank you for your participation. We hope you have a restful summer.

educational services. The rationale for the project was that these rural areas have limited access to health care because of a shortage of health care providers, so telemedicine was being used to deliver services to these underserved regions. There were two major thrusts for the project: to deliver health care services using telemedicine, and to furnish education to the health care providers.

To deliver health care services, the first prong of the project, telemedicine was used. Telemedicine is a system that combines computer, video, and network communication technologies; it enables health care providers to deliver services to people at some distance from the provider. The system includes (but is not limited to) using videos so that the provider and patient can communicate, real-time transmission of x-rays of other digital images, and cameras used by surgeons applied to examination of any part of the body (for example, during laparoscopic surgery). The telemedicine services provided by the grantees included consultation for health care specialists in areas such as cardiology, psychiatry, pain management, infectious diseases, emergency medicine, and dermatology, using store-and-forward and computer-based video conferencing methods.

The educational efforts, the second prong of the project, stemmed from three related issues: (1) turnover of medical staff in rural areas was high partly owing to the staff's limited professional development opportunities, (2) rural health care providers treat a broader scope of problems that are due to the limited number of specialists, and (3) there are fewer nurses trained at the bachelor's level in rural areas of the state than in urban centers. Distance-education courses were delivered in an attempt to reduce turnover and improve the skills of health care providers in these rural regions.

An external evaluation team was hired to assess the impact of ABC with regard to improving access to care and quality of services. When ABC and the ten grantees were funded, they were instructed that 5 percent of their funding was for working with the external evaluation team and that evaluation was part of their contractual agreement. The evaluation took place over a four-year period. Although it incorporated many evaluation methods, including interviews and document reviews, online surveys created using SurveyMonkey and Zoomerang were used throughout the process.

Needs Assessment. Online surveys were used for three-day telemedicine training courses to assess the needs of the registered attendees. While registering for the courses, people were required to complete the survey as part of their registration process. The questions included topics such as experience with telemedicine, educational needs, and demographic data such as length of time in position and professional title.

The course facilitators had access to the needs assessment results at any time because the data were part of the course registration process, it did not contain any confidential information, and the purpose of the survey was explained in the survey directions. This process enabled the facilitators to tailor their course to their audience; it was easy for course participants to complete the survey online while they were registering. Because completion of the survey was required for registration, the response rate was high, the respondents gave thoughtful answers and valuable information in their responses to the open-ended questions, and they answered all the questions. The outcome of using an online survey for this needs assessment was positive.

Process Evaluation. Online surveys for the process evaluation were used to assess the quality of ABC's technical assistance to the grantees. The technical assistance was related to ABC's support and capacity-building efforts. Grantees were e-mailed an online survey by the evaluation team, and a follow-up reminder was sent two weeks following the initial e-mail. All but one of the potential respondents completed the survey.

Online surveys also were used at the midpoint of the grant funding cycle. At that time, the evaluation team asked the grantees by e-mail to complete the survey. It was part of their contractual agreement, so the response rate was 100 percent and nearly all of the grantees completed the survey in great detail.

Online surveys were also used to assess the level of collaboration among the grantees. This was done twice, and the results were compared to see if the degree of collaboration increased. There were five levels of collaboration that the respondent could select. All of the grantees were listed in the left column, and a matrix was set up with headings giving each level of collaboration and an explanation of characteristics of each level below the heading. Other than introductory comments and directions, there was only one statement on the survey: "Using the scale provided, please indicate the extent to which you currently interact with each grantee." All of the grantees completed the survey in a timely fashion.

Internet surveys were also used to collect data from the grantees and measure progress throughout the grant cycle. Questions that were related to the number of consultations, type of consultation, and so on were gathered. The grantees had a choice of completing the surveys monthly or quarterly. This enabled the evaluation team to collect information during the grant process to measure progress, become aware of any problems the grantees were having, and gather data that would ultimately be used in the outcome component of the evaluation.

Outcome Evaluation. The outcome evaluation entailed use of paper and online surveys. For the three-day courses mentioned in the needs assessment, paper surveys were employed to conduct course evaluations. This was more practical than using an online survey because the target audience (course participants) was sitting in the classroom.

Similar to the midpoint online survey, online surveys were used at the end of the grant funding cycle. The same process was employed. Within fifteen days of the end of their funding cycle, the evaluation team e-mailed the grantee and asked them to complete the survey. The results resembled those of the midpoint survey. The response rate was 100 percent, and again nearly all the grantees completed the survey in great detail.

To measure patient and provider satisfaction, a paper version of the survey was distributed to the patients and providers at the time of service. This was a better option because they were not sitting in front of a computer when the services were provided; an online format would have required them to log on to the Internet and complete the survey. This approach would likely have resulted in a poor response rate; because of the demographics of the patient target population, the evaluation team was concerned they would not have Internet access. The completed paper surveys were faxed and mailed to the evaluation team by the staff member at the health care facility. These survey results were then entered into an online format for ease of data analysis and so that survey results could be shared immediately with the grantees.

Impact Evaluation. Internet-based surveys found use in the impact evaluation as well. For the three-day training courses, a three-month post-training online survey was e-mailed by the evaluation team to all of the course attendees. The online survey inquired about use and applicability of the course content and materials and any suggested changes to the curriculum. The response rate averaged approximately 40 percent. One follow-up reminder was sent two weeks after this initial e-mail request. The results were shared with the appropriate people at the organization using Zoomerang's restricted results option so that the identity of survey participants was not revealed.

Summary

Online surveys were a critical and effective component of the data collection process in both of the cases discussed in this chapter. For the university seeking to better serve its students, an online needs assessment survey of the freshman class produced information that helped the administration and student services providers efficiently plan programs and services for the school year. A follow-up outcome evaluation survey allowed the university to recontact participants from the needs assessment survey to investigate how well the newly tailored student services met the needs of the freshman class.

The telemedicine evaluation project used Internet-based surveys throughout the evaluation process. The online surveys were particularly valuable because the respondents were geographically dispersed (making other survey modes difficult if not impossible); furthermore, the evaluation team had access to the e-mail addresses of the target audience, rendering sampling a straightforward task. Even when the evaluation team did not have the addresses of the target audience, for example, online surveys were still useful in collecting patient and provider satisfaction data.

GLOSSARY

ALT tag (alternative text) provides a text description of the content of an image. It is used by text and audio browsers in place of an image.

Application service provider (ASP) a business that offers computer-based services to customers over a network.

Census data collected from the entire set of a population.

Cluster sample a sampling technique where the entire population is divided into groups, or clusters, and a random sample of these clusters are selected. All observations in the selected clusters are included in the sample.

Convenience sample a sample where the participants are selected, in part or as a whole, at the convenience of the evaluator.

Matched controls sample an intervention group matched with controls selected by the evaluator.

Sampling frame the list or other record of the population from which the sample is drawn.

SAS an acronym for Statistical Analysis System; software for statistical analysis of data.

Simple random sample a group of respondents (a sample) chosen from a larger group (a population). Every subject from the population has an equal probability of being chosen for the sample.

Snowball sample a technique for selecting a sample where existing study subjects recruit future subjects from among their acquaintances.

SPSS an acronym for Statistical Package for the Social Sciences; software for statistical analysis of data.

Stratified sample samples drawn from particular categories or strata of the population.

Systematic sample a sample obtained by taking every nth subject or case from a list of the population.

URL acronym for Uniform Resource Locator, the global address of documents and other resources on the World Wide Web.

Volunteer opt-in panel a group of people who have volunteered to participate in online surveys.

Wizard part of a computer program that guides users through steps in a process, such as writing letters, creating slide shows, or importing data from one software program into another.

INDEX

A
ABC telemedicine project case study: background information on, 61–62; impact evaluation during, 64; needs assessment during, 62–63; process and outcome evaluations during, 63–64
American Evaluation Association (AEA), ethical guiding principles developed by, 2, 11–15
Animation, 42
Anonymity issue, 12–13
Application service providers (ASPs). *See* Web-based survey hosts (or ASPs)
Attitude questions, 32

B
Behavioral questions, 31–32
Behavioral theory, 49
Budgets, 8
Button navigation, 40*fig*

C
Case studies: ABC telemedicine project, 61–64; university needs assessment—formative evaluation, 57–60*fig*; university needs assessment—summative evaluation, 60–61*t*. *See also* Online surveys
Check boxes, 43*fig*
Cleaning data, 51–53
Closed populations, 24
Colors, 41–42
Conducting online surveys: increasing response rate, 48–49; recruiting participants, 47–48
Confidentiality issue, 12–13
Contingency questions, 35*fig*
Couper, M. P., 28
Customer service, 22

D
Data: downloading and cleaning, 51–53; sharing the, 21; transforming, 53–54*fig*
Data analysis, 21
Data spreadsheet, 53–54*fig*
Demographic questions, 32–33
Dillman, D. A., 8, 37
Disseminating survey results: ethical interpretation and, 13–14; Web-based survey hosts capabilities for, 21
Downloading data, 51–53
Drop-down menus, 43*fig*–44

E
E-mail invitations: needs assessment survey follow-up, 61*fig*; recruitment using, 47–48

ERIC Clearinghouse on Assessment and Evaluation, 32
Ethical issues: AEA guiding principles on, 2, 11–13; informed consent, confidentiality, and anonymity, 11–13; interpretation and reporting of results, 13–14
Evaluation plan, 18
Evaluations: formative, 9*fig*–10, 57–60*t*; impact, 11, 64; outcomes, 10–11, 63–64; plan for, 18; process, 10, 63; steps in, 16*fig*; summative, 9*fig*, 10–11, 60–61*t*
Evaluators: AEA guiding principles on ethics for, 11; identifying the, 17; technological expertise of, 8–9; time frame and budget allowed, 8

F
Face-to-face interviewing, 6
Factual questions, 31
Formative evaluations: definition of, 9; online surveys used during, 9*fig*–10; university needs assessment case study, 57–60*t*
Formatting issues: color, 41–42; graphics and animation, 42; text, 41

G
Geographic locations of respondents, 7
Goals/objectives, 18
Graphics, 42

I
Impact evaluations: described, 11; telemedicine project case study, 64
Informed consent, 11–12
Instructions (questionnaire), 39
Intercept sampling, 26
Internet access, 7, 25
Item nonresponse, 27–28

K
Kittleson, M., 48
Knowledge Networks, 25

L
Likert-type scale, 32, 33*fig*
Links, 41
Listserv survey invitations, 48
Login screen, 38*fig*–39
Lumsden, J., 37

M
Mail surveys, 6
Mathison, S., 3

Matrix questions, 44*fig*
Microsoft Excel, 21
Morgan, W., 37
Multimethod sampling approach, 25
Multiple choice questions, 33, 34*fig*

N

Navigation: buttons used for, 40*fig*; links used for, 41; progress bars used for, 41*fig*
Needs assessments: case study on formative evaluation, 57–60*t*; case study on summative evaluation, 60–61*fig*; described, 9–10; telemedicine project case study, 62–63
Newsgroup survey invitations, 48
Nonprobability samples: described, 26; sample size issue of, 27
Nonresponse bias, 27–28
Numerical codes, 53, 54*fig*

O

Objectives. *See* Goals/objectives
Online survey factors: evaluator, 8–9, 11, 17; questionnaire, 7–8, 37–45; respondent, 6–7, 11–13, 25, 27–28
Online survey planning: determining the resources, 17–18; as evaluation process step, 16*fig*; identifying an evaluator, 17; identifying/engaging the stakeholders, 17; selecting software for your evaluation project, 18–22; writing the evaluation plan, 18; writing goals and objectives, 18
Online surveys: advantages of, 5; appropriate use of, 6–9; conducting, 47–50; ethical issues of, 11–14; examining appropriate use of, 1–2; increasing use of, 1; during various stages of evaluation, 9*fig*–11. *See also* Case studies
Open populations, 24
Open-ended question, 35*fig*–36
Open-text boxes, 44*fig*
Outcome evaluations: described, 10–11; telemedicine project case study, 63–64

P

Participants: informed consent of, 11–12; recruiting, 47–48; sampling frame of, 7. *See also* Respondents; Samples
Password protection/security, 22
Pilot testing, 10
Populations: definition of, 23; open and closed, 24; selecting samples representative of, 24
Postal mail surveys, 6
Prerecruited panels, 25
Pretesting questionnaires, 44–45
Probability samples, 25–26
Process evaluation: described, 10; telemedicine project case study, 63
Progress bars, 41*fig*

Q

Question types: attitude, 32; about behavior, 31–32; demographic, 32–33; factual, 31; Likert-type scale, 32, 33*fig*; overview of, 7–8

Question writing guidelines: for clear questions, 29–30; for relevant questions, 30–31; for short questions, 30; for unbiased questions, 30
Questionnaire organization: instructions, 39; layout, 40; login screen, 38*fig*–39; navigation, 40*fig*–41*fig*; questions, 39; thank you, 40; welcome, 37–38*fig*
Questionnaires: formatting, 41–42; nature and length of questions in, 8, 39; organization of, 37–41*fig*; pretesting, 44–45; response formats used on, 33–36, 42–44; types of questions included in, 7–8, 31–33
Questions: designing online survey, 7–8; guidelines for writing, 29–31; matrix, 44*fig*; nature and length of, 8, 39; numerical codes for, 53, 54*fig*; order of, 39; response format of, 33–36, 42–44; sensitive, 39; types of online, 7–8, 31–33

R

Radio buttons, 42*fig*–43
Random-digit dialing, 25
Ranking questions, 34*fig*–35
Rating scale question, 33–34*fig*
Read Regular font, 41
Recruiting participants, 47–48
Relevant questions, 30–31
Reporting results: ethical interpretation and, 13–14; Web-based survey hosts capabilities for, 21
Resources: determining the, 17–18; online survey budget, 8
Respondents: anonymity/confidentiality issues for, 12–13; increasing rate of response by, 48–49; informed consent of, 11–12; Internet access by, 7, 25; nonresponse by, 27–28; sampling frame of, 7. *See also* Participants; Samples
Respondents geographic location of, 7
Response format: check boxes, 43*fig*; contingency questions, 35*fig*; drop-down menu, 43*fig*–44; matrix questions, 44*fig*; multiple choice, 33, 34*fig*; open-ended question, 35*fig*–36; open-text boxes, 44*fig*; radio buttons, 42*fig*–43; ranking, 34*fig*–35; rating scales, 33–34*fig*
Response rates, 48–49
Ritter, L. A., 3, 22

S

Samples: nonprobability, 26; nonresponse bias, 27–28; for online surveys, 24–26; populations and representative, 23–24; probability, 25–26; size of, 26–27. *See also* Participants; Respondents
Sampling frame, 7
SAS, 21
Schaefer, R., 8
Scholastic Aptitude Test (SAT), 59
Security/password protection, 22
Sensitive questions, 39
Short questions, 30
Springette, J., 9
SPSS, 21
Stakeholders: identifying and engaging the, 17; sharing data with, 21

STATPAC, 21
Sue, V. M., 3, 22
Summative evaluations: definition of, 9*fig*, 10; online survey used during, 10–11; university needs assessment case study, 60–61*fig*
SurveyMonkey, 18, 21, 51, 52*fig*
SurveyMonkey's Basic Results Report, 52*fig*

T

Technical expertise (evaluator), 8–10
Telemedicine project. *See* ABC telemedicine project case study
Telephone surveys, 6
Text fonts, 41
Thank you screen, 40
Time frame, 8
Transforming data, 53–54*fig*

U

Unbiased questions, 30
Unit nonresponse, 27

University needs assessment: formative evaluation case study, 57–60*fig*; summative evaluation case study, 60–61*t*

W

Web presence, 48
Web-based survey hosts (or ASPs): access for all/multiple users, 22; cost of, 19–20; data analysis capabilities, 21; data spreadsheet from, 54*fig*; described, 18–19; disseminating your survey, 21; issues related to questions/response options, 20; limitation and appearance of, 20; sample of online survey vendors, 19*t*; sampling options, 20–21; security and customer service of, 22; sharing data, 21; user-friendliness of, 20
WebSurvey, 22
Welcome screen, 37–38*fig*

Z

Zoomerang, 18, 21

New Directions for Evaluation
Order Form
SUBSCRIPTIONS AND SINGLE ISSUES

DISCOUNTED BACK ISSUES:

Use this form to receive **20% off** all back issues of New Directions for Evaluation. All single issues priced at **$21.60** (normally $27.00).

TITLE   ISSUE NO.   ISBN

_____   _____   _____
_____   _____   _____
_____   _____   _____

Call 888-378-2537 or see mailing instructions below. When calling, mention the promotional code, JB7ND, to receive your discount.

SUBSCRIPTIONS: (1 year, 4 issues)

☐ New Order   ☐ Renewal

U.S.	☐ Individual: $80	☐ Institutional: $199
Canada/Mexico	☐ Individual: $80	☐ Institutional: $239
All Others	☐ Individual: $104	☐ Institutional: $273

Call 888-378-2537 or see mailing and pricing instructions below. Online subscriptions are available at www.interscience.wiley.com.

Copy or detach page and send to:
**John Wiley & Sons, Journals Dept, 5th Floor
989 Market Street, San Francisco, CA 94103-1741**

Order Form can also be faxed to: 888-481-2665

Issue/Subscription Amount: $ _____
Shipping Amount: $ _____
(for single issues only—subscription prices include shipping)
Total Amount: $ _____

SHIPPING CHARGES:
SURFACE   Domestic   Canadian
First Item $5.00 $6.00
Each Add'l Item $3.00 $1.50

(No sales tax for U.S. subscriptions. Canadian residents, add GST for subscription orders. Individual rate subscriptions must be paid by personal check or credit card. Individual rate subscriptions may not be resold as library copies.)

☐ Payment enclosed (U.S. check or money order only. All payments must be in U.S. dollars.)
☐ VISA ☐ MC ☐ Amex # _____ Exp. Date _____
Card Holder Name _____ Card Issue # _____
Signature _____ Day Phone _____
☐ Bill Me (U.S. institutional orders only. Purchase order required.)
Purchase order # _____
          Federal Tax ID13559302   GST 89102 8052
Name _____
Address _____
Phone _____ E-mail _____

JB7ND

Other Titles Available

NEW DIRECTIONS FOR EVALUATION
Sandra Mathison, Editor-in-Chief

For a complete list of back issues, please visit www.josseybass.com/go/ev

EV 114   **Enduring Issues in Evaluation: The 20th Anniversary of the Collaboration between NDE and AEA**
Sandra Mathison
This issue of *New Directions for Evaluation* looks back at the past twenty years of the American Evaluation Association, from its inception to current research, highlighting important moments and enduring issues in the discipline and profession of evaluation. The issue includes a very brief history of NDE—including the journal's purpose, the various foci, how the journal has operated, and such events as the change in the journal's name. The issue also looks at the substance of NDE over the past twenty years, including an analysis of the coverage of cultural diversity issues. But much of the issue is devoted to "greatest hits" chapters that have appeared in prior NDE issues, each of which is introduced by an analysis of what makes it a significant contribution to the evaluation literature.
ISBN 978-04701-7900-0

EV 113   **Informing Federal Policies on Evaluation Methodology: Building the Evidence Base for Method Choice in Government Sponsored Evaluation**
George Julnes, Debra J. Rog, Editors
This volume seeks to provide a space for a more productive dialogue that, by identifying areas of agreement but also fundamental differences, will promote a more durable working consensus on the circumstances in which some methods are to be preferred over others. The chapter authors and discussants make clear that there are different types of evidence with which to inform this dialogue, including empirical findings of the impact of method choice on evaluation outcomes, the evidence contained in the wisdom of practice, and the results of critical analyses of the broader social impacts of method choice. The editors build on these contributions to suggest pragmatic policies for federal agencies, promoting both context-appropriate method choice and the importance of managing portfolios of evaluative research that maintain desired distributions of methodologies.
ISBN 978-07879-97342

EV 112   Promoting the Use of Government Evaluations in Policymaking
Rakesh Mohan, Kathleen Sullivan, Editors
This volume explores management of the politics of evaluation, which can be accomplished by considering the context in which an evaluation occurs and examining strategies for maximizing both evaluators' independence from and their responsiveness to key stakeholders. Unconventional approaches, such as prospective evaluation and development of analytical tools for use by agency personnel, are examined, as is promotion of evaluation use through a symbiotic relationship with performance measurement. The chapter authors discuss utilization strategies as applied to evaluations of public health, education, and corrections programs. The final chapter provides sage advice to evaluators on how to impact policy development.
ISBN 978-07879-97083

EV 111   Independent Evaluation Consulting
Gail V. Barrington, Dawn Hanson Smart, Editors
Inspired by conversations among independent consultants at the annual conferences of the American Evaluation Association (AEA), this volume examines topics unique to independent consulting, representing day-to-day realities and challenges that span the consultant's career. In examining these topics, contributors explore ways in which these evaluators think about, approach, and implement evaluation. There has never before been a compilation that addresses these issues unique to independent consulting. With the burgeoning interest in independent consulting, this topic is timely and should serve as a springboard to ongoing discussion among evaluators.
ISBN 978-07879-95591

EV 110   Pitfalls and Pratfalls: Null and Negative Findings in Evaluating Interventions
Cynthia Hudley, Robert Nash Parker, Editors
This volume examines the problem of null or negative evaluation findings, a topic rarely discussed in the literature but all too commonplace in the experience of evaluators. The Southern California Center of Excellence on Youth Violence Prevention, housed in the Robert Presley Center for Crime and Justice Studies at the University of California, Riverside, has taken up the challenge to discuss candidly evaluation efforts that can be described only as challenging. The individual chapters discuss a range of design, implementation, and analysis issues relevant not only to evaluation studies but also to interventions that can contribute to negative or null findings in the evaluation of an

intervention program. These problems that are the realities of life for anyone who conducts prevention and intervention research are typically the stuff of research seminar comments and barroom digressions late in the evening at professional meetings. This issue brings those important lessons into the larger discussion that will influence prevention science and public policy. The contributors to this volume not only admit a set of problems and shortcomings but also attempt to draw general lessons, cautions, and advice for those who evaluate prevention and intervention efforts.
ISBN 978-07879-88289

EV 109 **Critical Issues in STEM Evaluation**
Douglass Huffman, Frances Lawrenz
This volume of *New Directions for Evaluation* focuses on evaluation of science, technology, engineering, and mathematics (STEM) programs, with special emphasis on evaluation of STEM education initiatives. STEM evaluation has always been important, given the issues facing public schools and the economic and social considerations of STEM fields. But because these fields today face a variety of concerns, this discussion of STEM evaluation is particularly timely. Evaluation advances may contribute to STEM fields by helping programs address the challenges they face. This volume presents multiple viewpoints and state-of-the-art examples and methodological approaches in the hope that its chapters will contribute to the understanding of STEM evaluation, STEM education, STEM education evaluation, and evaluation in general. Overall, this volume of *New Directions for Evaluation* may help not only to move the field to consider new methods and methodologies for engaging in evaluation but also to reconsider ideas of what it means to engage in scientific evaluation.
ISBN 978-07879-85882

EV 108 **Evaluating Nonformal Education Programs and Settings**
Emma Norland, Cindy Somers, Editors
This volume explores the issues with which evaluators of nonformal education programs (such as parks, zoos, community outreach organizations, and museums) struggle. These issues are not unique to nonformal programs and settings. Rather, they pose different sets of problems and solutions from those that face evaluators of traditional education programs. The authors address this topic from extensive experience as evaluators and education professionals who have worked in nonformal education settings.
ISBN 978-07879-85424

EV 107   **Social Network Analysis in Program Evaluation**
Maryann M. Durland, Kimberly A Fredericks, Editors
This important issue of *New Directions for Evaluation* highlights social network analysis (SNA) methodology and its application within program evaluation. The application of SNA is relatively new for mainstream evaluation, and like most other innovations, it has yet to be fully explored in this field. The volume aims to fill the gaps within SNA methodology exploration by first reviewing the foundations and development of network analysis within the social sciences and the field of evaluation. The focus then turns to the methodology. Who holds power in a network, and what measures indicate whether that power is direct or indirect? Which subgroups have formed, and where are they positioned in an organization? How divided is an organization? Who forms the core of a collaboration, and where are the experts in an organization? These are the types of common questions explored in the four case studies of the use of network analysis within an evaluative framework. These cases are diverse in their evaluation situations and in the application of measures, providing a basis to model common applications of network analysis within the field. The final chapters include a personal account of current use by a government agency and suggestions for the future use of SNA for evaluation practice.
ISBN 978-07879-83949

EV 106   **Theorists' Models in Action**
Marvin Alkin, Christina A. Christie, Editors
This volume analyzes how evaluation theorists apply their approach in practice. A scenario of a situation at an elementary school is presented to four prominent theorists, who describe how they would design and conduct an evaluation of the school's program. The editors consider the theorists' proposed evaluations, as well as their subsequent comments, to develop themes related to the influence of theory and context on practice. They also provide a comparative analysis of the theorists' evaluation approaches in relation to the context of evaluation case presented. This volume demonstrates why evaluators need to adapt their point of view to a particular situation, and provides much-needed study and analysis on the way in which they make those adaptations.
ISBN 978-07879-82126

EV 105   **Teaching Evaluation Using the Case Method**
Michael Quinn Patton, Patricia Patrizi, Editors
The absence of readily available teaching cases has been a significant gap in the field of evaluation. This volume aims to

begin filling that gap by presenting high-quality evaluation cases developed specifically for use with the case method. The volume begins by reviewing evaluation issues that cases can be used to surface and provides guidance for using the case method. Three in-depth cases are then presented for quite different evaluation situations. Each has been taught, field-tested, and refined in line with participant feedback. Each case ends with teaching questions and key evaluation points those questions are aimed at elucidating. Following the case chapters, a professional evaluator reflects on his experiences with the cases and offers lessons learned about evaluation teaching and training, including exercises for extrapolating lessons, illuminating ethical dilemmas, understanding and applying alternative evaluation models, and conducting metaevaluations, among other uses.
ISBN 978-07879-80160

EV 104   **International Perspectives on Evaluation Standards**
Craig Russon, Gabrielle Russon, Editors
Prior to 1995, there were fewer than half a dozen regional and national evaluation organizations around the world. Today there are more than fifty, attesting to a growing interest in the practice of program evaluation internationally. Many of these new organizations have undertaken efforts to develop their own standards or to modify existing sets—most typically, the Program Evaluation Standards of the Joint Committee on Standards for Educational Evaluation—for use in their own cultural context. Following two introductory chapters, one a conceptual overview and the second a history of the development and revisions of the Program Evaluation Standards, this issue documents standards development efforts in three different settings: Western Europe, Africa, and Australasia. In addition, because nongovernmental organizations and governments have entered the standard-setting business, other chapters describe standards development activities by the European Commission and CARE International. The content points to the challenge of formalizing standards for program evaluation given cross-cultural differences in values and to the continuing challenges related to implementing voluntary standards.
ISBN 978-07879-78587

EV 103   **Global Advances in HIV/AIDS Monitoring and Evaluation**
Deborah Rugg, Greet Peersman, Michael Carael
The focus of this issue is on global advances in conducting monitoring and evaluation (M&E) of the global response to the

HIV/AIDS epidemic. Only by implementing comprehensive and sustainable M&E systems will we know how much progress we are making, as nations and as a global community, in combating this pandemic. The chapters primarily focus on developing nations and are presented largely from the perspective of evaluators working for donors, international agencies, and national governments. Although it is clear that a comprehensive M7E system must eventually include both monitoring and evaluation, the initial aim has been to establish a foundation derived largely from surveys and monitoring information. To date, much of the focus in M&E has come from the global level because new global funding intiatives been launched and required rapid scale-up and the development of technical guidance, international standards, and indicators for monitoring progress and determining success. At the regional and country levels, the challenge has been to implement national M&E plans and systems within a context of overall low M&E capacity and a range of M&E needs.
ISBN 978-07879-77801

EV 102   **In Search of Cultural Competence in Evaluation: Toward Principles and Practice**
Melva Thompson-Robinson, Rodney Hopson, Saumitra SenGupta, Editors
This volume focuses on culturally competent evaluation. The chapters address a number of questions: How does culture matter in evaluation theory and practice? How does attention to cultural issues make for better evaluation practice? How does attention to cultural issues make for better evaluation practice? What is the "value-addedness" of cultural competence in evaluation? How do the complexities, challenges, and politics of diversity issue affect evaluation? The first chapter is an overview of culture, cultural competence, and culturally competent evaluation; the other chapters provide case studies on the implementation of culturally competent evaluation in a variety of settings and with several populations. The volume contributors also present lessons learned from their experiences and recommendations for implementing cultural competent evaluations in general. This volume is part of an important discussion of race, culture, and diversity in evaluation striving to shape and advance culturally competent evaluation, and, in tandem, evaluation of culturally competent services.
ISBN 978-07879-76545

**NEW DIRECTIONS FOR EVALUATION
IS NOW AVAILABLE ONLINE AT WILEY INTERSCIENCE**

What is Wiley InterScience?

Wiley InterScience is the dynamic online content service from John Wiley & Sons delivering the full text of over 300 leading scientific, technical, medical, and professional journals, plus major reference works, the acclaimed Current Protocols laboratory manuals, and even the full text of select Wiley print books online.

What are some special features of Wiley InterScience?

Wiley Interscience Alerts is a service that delivers table of contents via e-mail for any journal available on Wiley InterScience as soon as a new issue is published online.

Early View is Wiley's exclusive service presenting individual articles online as soon as they are ready, even before the release of the compiled print issue. These articles are complete, peer-reviewed, and citable.

CrossRef is the innovative multi-publisher reference linking system enabling readers to move seamlessly from a reference in a journal article to the cited publication, typically located on a different server and published by a different publisher.

How can I access Wiley InterScience?

Visit http://www.interscience.wiley.com.

Guest Users can browse Wiley InterScience for unrestricted access to journal Tables of Contents and Article Abstracts, or use the powerful search engine.
Registered Users are provided with a *Personal Home Page* to store and manage customized alerts, searches, and links to favorite journals and articles. Additionally, Registered Users can view free Online Sample Issues and preview selected material from major reference works.
Licensed Customers are entitled to access full-text journal articles in PDF, with select journals also offering full-text HTML.

How do I become an Authorized User?

Authorized Users are individuals authorized by a paying Customer to have access to the journals in Wiley InterScience. For example, a University that subscribes to Wiley journals is considered to be the Customer.
Faculty, staff and students authorized by the University to have access to those journals in Wiley InterScience are Authorized Users. Users should contact their Library for information on which Wiley journals they have access to in Wiley InterScience.

ASK YOUR INSTITUTION ABOUT WILEY INTERSCIENCE TODAY!